Road to Relevance

5 Strategies for Competitive Associations

HARRISON COERVER AND MARY BYERS, CAE

The Center for Association Leadership

WASHINGTON, DC

ASAE: The Center for Association Leadership
1575 I Street, NW
Washington, DC 20005-1103
Phone: 202-371-0940 (when calling from within the Washington, D.C. metropolitan area)
Phone: 888-950-2723 (when calling from outside the Washington, D.C. metropolitan area)
Fax: 202-220-6439
Email: books@asaecenter.org

ASAE: The Center for Association Leadership connect great ideas to great people to inspire leadership and achievement within the association community.

Keith C. Skillman, CAE, Vice President, Publications, ASAE: The Center for Association Leadership
Baron Williams, CAE, Director, Book Publishing, ASAE: The Center for Association Leadership

A complete catalog of ASAE titles is available online at www.asaecenter.org/bookstore.

Cover design by Beth Lower
Interior design by Cimarron Design, cimarrondesign.com

International Standard Book Number, 10 digit: 0-88034-356-7
International Standard Book Number, 13 digit: 978-0-88034-356-5

Printed in the United States of America.
10 9 8 7 6 5 4 3 2

Contents

Foreword

This is a book about competition. It's a book about how your association can perform well despite the onslaught of unprecedented, ubiquitous, and relentless competition in the space that once belonged exclusively to associations. And it's a book about the "new normal" facing today's associations.

Even before the Great Recession of 2008, associations were challenged by a convergence of fundamental changes in markets, member preferences, and technology. Call *Road to Relevance* a guidebook, a playbook, or a handbook, its purpose is to equip association executives and volunteers with guidance in strategic thinking and, more importantly, strategic acting in the world of association management.

We define strategy as "the skillful, creative, and disciplined use of an organization's resources to achieve its objectives." In essence, this book is all about how to optimize the association's resources in very challenging and changing times.

To be successful, strategies have to fit an organization's industry dynamics and market conditions and take into account internal functioning and capabilities. In their article, "Your Strategy Needs a Strategy," Reeves, Love, and Tillmanns call this "matching strategy-making process to the specific demands of competitive environments."[1] Accordingly, we have identified the five strategic concepts that we are convinced are the right ones to prescribe for trade associations and professional societies today. They aren't new. As a matter of fact, they have been around for years. What is new is their application to the way associations are governed and managed.

Strategy becomes a multiplier for your association when you narrow your attention and determine to do fewer things—and to do them with excellence. It's the same concept that today's most successful for-profit companies use—and one you can adapt to ensure your association's future.

In the quest to create a winning value proposition, the average association is trying to be too many things to too many people, thereby reducing its significance and increasing the chances of irrelevance. Yet, as Peter Drucker writes, "Wherever we find a business that is outstandingly successful, we will find that it has thought through the concentration alternatives and has made a concentration decision."[2] He also notes, "The worst thing to do is a little bit of everything. This makes sure that nothing is being accomplished. It is better to pick the wrong priority than none at all."[3]

While we wouldn't recommend picking the wrong priority, we do agree that it is dangerous to pick none at all. We've seen this failure time and time again in our work with more than 1,400 trade and professional organizations. Yet "business as usual" no longer produces the same results and the uncertainty of "business as unusual" keeps many organizations stuck.

In our first book, *Race for Relevance: 5 Radical Changes for Associations*, we identified the six challenges that have changed forever the environment for associations. We also suggested five radical changes to ensure future relevance and success. We know we hit a nerve. We receive emails and calls almost daily asking, "Did you write this about *our* association?"

The radical changes have certainly provoked thought, discussion, deliberation, and in some cases, disagreement. We're gratified by the discourse. Like Peter Drucker, who believes it's better to pick the wrong priority than none at all, we believe it's better to have an honest conversation about an association's future—however difficult this may be—than not to talk at all. In many cases, these discussions have ended with a question: "We know we need to do something, but what—and how?"

This book answers the "what" and "how." We identify five practical, realistic strategies for your organization and share how to implement them. You'll learn how to:

- Build on strength;
- Concentrate resources;
- Integrate programs and services;
- Align people and processes for efficiency;
- Abandon services and activities when necessary.

Road to Relevance is designed for association professionals and volunteer leaders alike. Part primer, part field manual, it includes adaptable examples from the for-profit world and case studies of successful associations that have applied the concepts in the book—and are succeeding as a result. Though it is not necessary to be familiar with our first book, *Race for Relevance,* the two books are written as companion guides. *Road to Relevance* begins where *Race for Relevance* ends. Both help generate conversation and possibility thinking for staff and leaders. Both books help you identify what's most significant—and, therefore, meaningful—about what you offer members. And both provide roadmaps for those leading both professional societies and trade groups.

We know that strategy is difficult. It's more fun to chase after a new idea or the latest management fad, but successful organizations purposely don't do that. And that's what makes them successful. It takes great discipline and determination to harness the power of focus to implement strategy.

The bottom line: Associations that focus on helping members work less stressfully, more productively, and more profitably will remain competitive. Those that don't will simply be a footnote in the annals of history—such as the Textile Distributors Association; the International Cake, Candy & Party Supply Association; and the Community Broadcasters Association.

We challenge you to have the courage to adapt the strategies in this book. They lead to new thinking, clearer decisions, and effective planning. More than anything, they lead to a relevant association that successfully competes in the "new normal."

CHAPTER ONE

The New Normal

*"It is increasingly clear that the current downturn is
fundamentally different from recessions of recent decades.
We are experiencing not merely another turn of the
business cycle, but a restructuring of the economic order."*
— Ian Davis[4]

Our jobs as consultants put us in board rooms, off-site retreats, and
strategy sessions week in and week out. Between us, we've worked with
more than 1,400 not-for-profit organizations. Though the locations
and associations vary, we hear similar comments and questions. That's
how our first book, *Race for Relevance*, came to be. When we started to
hear the same concerns and comments from a wide variety of associations—whether they served dentists, physicians, plumbers, engineers,
veterinarians, attorneys, car and truck dealers, law enforcement officials,
convenience store owners, nurses, manufacturers, school principals, or
bankers—we began to pay attention. The more we listened, the more
convinced we became that the patterns we were seeing were actually
a fundamental shift that led to what we call the new normal, based on
six challenges facing today's associations. We also proposed five radical
changes and outlined them in *Race for Relevance*.

Although the two books are complementary, you need not have read *Race to Relevance* to fully understand *Road to Relevance.* In case you haven't read *Race,* the following is a brief review of the challenges it outlined:

1. Time Pressures

The traditional association model is time intensive. We ask members to take time to serve on a board or committee, to read our publications and e-blasts, and to attend the annual meeting and continuing education programs. Yet people are busier than ever before. They work longer hours managing two-income households and juggling busy schedules. They fight for time for family, friends, and recreation, and they are examining their commitments more closely than ever.

Because the current association model requires a large time commitment, the pressures on members' time should be a concern. In fact, one Realtor® executive shared with us that when nonrenewing members were called, they used to say, "I can't afford the dues." Now she hears, "I didn't have time to access your programs and services." This shift should be a significant concern.

2. Value Expectations

In the "good ol' days" of association management, membership in a professional society was considered part of being a professional. Company membership in a trade association was considered an obligation. In the past, people and companies belonged because it was the "right thing to do." Members sent in their dues. Nobody asked any questions. No more. Individuals and companies expect return on their dues investment. The pressure on associations to demonstrate value has increased, and it is not going away.

3. Member Market Structure

All member markets are dynamic and over time most have undergone significant changes. Some have been rapidly transformed. (Consider how radically banking changed in the recession, for example.) Many associations are struggling to serve member markets that are vastly different from those they were initially designed to serve. Industry consolidation trends (such as what has occurred in publishing and education) and professional specialization (as in medicine and accounting) require a rigorous rethinking of the member market the association can competitively serve—and a look at whether today's members will even be around in a decade.

4. Generational Differences

While stereotyping is dangerous, it's clear that each generation has its own values. According to the 2006 report, "Generations and the Future of Association Participation," the difference between Generation X and Baby Boomers is "not in the propensity to join associations but in their expectations about what membership means and the return it provides."[5] Almost all our association clients express concerns about attracting and engaging young professionals and new entrants into the field. The association disconnect with each succeeding generation is real and growing.

5. Competition

In the past, most associations played in their own sandboxes with little competition. That competition-free environment is gone. The number of associations serving industries and professions has grown dramatically, resulting in increased association versus association competition. Competition from the for-profit sector has increased for virtually every association offering, from publications to trade shows to educational programs. Competition from the internet has been a game changer. Associations' ability (or lack thereof) to compete with a wide range of product and service providers is a new and considerable challenge.

6. Technology

A tidal wave of technologies has evolved to offer virtually every association deliverable and function: education, information, networking, fundraising, grassroots mobilization, and more. Associations were slow to adopt technology as the internet age dawned in the early 1990s, and their relevance is increasingly at risk if they don't bridge the resulting gap. Effectively responding to the potential of technologies that didn't exist just a few years ago is a major challenge for slow, reactive association practices.

If the Shoe Fits...

Which of the above challenges are affecting your association? Take a minute to rank them. Which appear highest on your list? Is it generational issues? Market specialization or consolidation? Time pressures? Whatever you ranked highest, know that these six challenges are increasingly and more rapidly making it difficult for associations to provide relevant value propositions and harder for members to find the time to take advantage of this value in a meaningful way. No association is immune, but some are challenged more directly than others.

Radical Change

We don't see the impact of the above challenges ending anytime soon. In fact, we see acceleration in the pressures on today's associations. Here are the radical changes we proposed to address the above issues. (To understand them and to learn how to start a conversation with your board about them, we recommend reading *Race for Relevance* if you haven't already done so. Many clients have told us their entire board has read the book and had productive discussions about it.)

1. Overhaul the Governance Model.

Associations need boards composed for performance, not boards composed according to geography, special interest, who one knows, or how long they've been hanging around. We need boards that can govern—direct and control—the association, not micromanage or mismanage it. We believe a smaller, competency-based board, with directors carefully selected for competencies critical to the organization's future, can be more effective. A radical idea? Not really. In practice, many associations are actually governed by a similarly sized executive committee. Why not just make that reality the official board?

2. Empower the CEO and Enhance Staff Expertise.

A successful association cannot afford to underuse its human capital, whether it be volunteer leaders or staff members. All should be operating at the highest and best use of their time and expertise. They should not be wasting time in board meetings, in unfocused committee meetings, or on projects or tasks that don't add to the member value proposition. The association that fails to optimize its CEO and staff is not in a competitive mode. In particular, the CEO is in a key role and must have the support of the board in managing the association in challenging times.

3. Rigorously Define the Member Market.

Too many associations are structured to serve a market that doesn't exist anymore. Take medicine, for example. The American Medical Association, founded in 1847, originally represented self-employed doctors, mostly solo-practitioners. Today, few medical school graduates will ever own their own practices. Instead, they will work for a corporate-owned entity, in a clinic or large healthcare system. The days of associations' ability to serve broad, sprawling member markets are over. Associations cannot be the equivalent of the obsolete department store in a retail industry with specialty stores, discounters, manufacturer's outlets, category killers, and online operators. Associations need a disciplined analysis of their member markets as they exist today and are likely to evolve tomorrow.

4. Rationalize Programs and Services.

The typical association tries to do too much. For most, the underlying thinking is that the more programs, services, products, and activities offered the more valuable membership is. Unfortunately, volume does not equal value. Associations should purposely concentrate their resources on a limited number of key programs and activities and should eliminate those that are obsolete, underperforming, or no longer relevant. By abandoning the losers, associations can allocate more resources to the winners. A benefit of a narrow product line is the improved ability to promote a few strong programs versus a long laundry list of "stuff."

5. Bridge the Technology Gap.

For most associations, investments in technology have been made slowly and grudgingly. A new mindset must acknowledge the promise of technology and how it will be critical in positioning associations in the future. Capitalizing on technology is not an option for associations. It is an imperative. Ignoring it is a shortcut to irrelevance.

The Future Starts Now

The association landscape has changed. What is your organization doing about it? It's foolhardy to hope the winds of change will take us back to the kinder and gentler days of the past. And it's downright delusional to think your association hasn't been, or won't be, affected. We bet you're already seeing the effects: member loss, declining participation in programs and services, and decreases in nondues revenue. Whether you care to admit it or not, it's happening. And it's not likely going to change anytime soon. Read what Ian Davis, McKinsey & Company's worldwide managing director, has to say:

> For some organizations, near-term survival is the only agenda item. Others are peering through the fog of uncertainty, thinking about how to position themselves once the crisis has passed and things return to normal. The question is, "What will normal look like?" While no one can say how long the crisis will last, what we find on the other side will not look like the normal of recent years. The new normal will be shaped by a confluence of powerful forces—some arising directly from the financial crisis and *some that were at work long before it began.* (Emphasis added.)[6]

There Is Hope

Whether you are an association CEO, staff member, or a volunteer leader, your association's story can have a happy ending. One of the best parts of our job is seeing a group of individuals set aside their own agendas and put their hearts and minds together to ensure the success of an organization, profession, or industry. We've seen some gutsy, game-changing decisions and some fabulous achievements, which we'll share in these pages.

What do the successful associations have in common? They are structured correctly. They have the right leaders and staff in place. They have a narrowly focused value proposition for a carefully identified market. They are leveraging technology. They are disciplined. And they are strategic. Read on to find how you can be, too.

CHAPTER TWO

Build on Strength

> *"There is great solace in the simple fact of*
> *clarity—about what is vital, and what is not."*
> — JIM COLLINS[7]

The challenges confronting associations in the new normal environment are considerable. And this challenging environment requires associations to be more focused, more competitive, and considerably more adept at using resources.

Operating in the new normal is not going to be easy for most associations. Tradition is the master of most associations. "The way we've always done it" sets the tone. But let's be honest: Many associations are run more like clubs than businesses, making it difficult, if not impossible, to make the necessary adjustments to thrive in the new normal environment.

We want to be clear: We recognize the unique nature of not-for-profits. We work almost exclusively with them. In our work, which spans decades, we've seen a shift. Today's thriving associations are more entrepreneurial and are adopting strategies previously seen in for-profit companies. Though profit isn't a driving motive for most associations, business strategies help strengthen organizations and often provide vital financial resources. And where they don't provide financial resources, they at least promote a "don't lose money" viewpoint—certainly a healthy perspective in challenging economic times.

The new normal involves an environment of more competition from more players—many nontraditional and unexpected. This increasingly competitive atmosphere demands new ways of thinking about how we govern and manage. Thus, the five strategies in this book. The first strategy for associations to embrace on the road to relevance is to build on their most significant strength.

The Crucial Importance of Building on Strength

Association boards often do an inadequate job of directing the association in a way that builds on strength, often because of lack of collective experience in strategy deployment. Board decisions are rarely supported by a rigorous assessment of what the association's strength is and how it can be leveraged for maximum performance and competitive advantage.

Some association CEOs follow the well-intentioned but often flawed leads of their part-time, time-pressed boards, many of which meet only twice a year. Rather than operating with a strength-based focus, associations attempt ventures for which they are ill equipped to succeed. They offer sprawling assortments of programs and services, few—or none—of which really excel in the marketplace. Others squander scarce resources in marginal activities that add little or no value. Still others zigzag from one president's priorities to the next. Instead of focusing on the association's strength, they chase the current leader's vision for his or her year, ensuring an operational strategy of two steps forward, one step back. Others don't even know what their strengths are or underestimate those they have. As Jean Van Rensselar writes in *Distributor Focus:*

> Most organizations tend to take things they do best for granted. They either assume that their competitors are doing the same things just as well or they underestimate the value of their strengths.
>
> Developing your organization's natural strengths is like launching a spaceship. Once you get off the ground—once your capabilities start to pull you out of the pack of competitors—those capabilities will continue to evolve and pull you further and further away with less and less effort. This is assuming that you strategically guard, nurture, and expand those capabilities.[8]

By failing to fully exploit their strength, associations drift away from their core assets and resources, often taking them for granted or, worse, failing to even identify them. The usual result is undertaking initiatives or programs the association is ill suited to perform.

Think about the culture of associations. Volunteers are recruited to "do" something for the organization. Often, they do so without clear guidance or direction from the board or staff (a frustration we hear frequently when we work with committees). When direction is given, it doesn't always reflect any carefully derived strategy.

Since more than a few directors on association boards believe their role is to come up with new ventures, new initiatives, or new undertakings for the association to pursue, everybody wants to come up with a new service, additional benefit, or the next "big thing." Year after year of this behavior culminates in a poorly thought out menu of services that rarely optimizes the association's strength. Think of a restaurant with a different manager each year who adds his or her favorite item to the menu. What would it look like in 10 years, 20 years? As we've noted, the process often takes the association into areas where the organization has little position, little expertise, and little chance of success.

In addition to the "doing" trap, associations fall into copying competitors: The Widget Manufacturers Association has a marketing program that promotes the use of member company widgets. We should have a public relations initiative that promotes the gizmos that our members produce. And off we go into the wild blue yonder of a product promotion campaign without a serious discussion of whether this is something that builds on the association's strength—or whether we have adequate financial resources or access to the necessary expertise. (Note: In regard to product promotion, just because association volunteers see, hear, or read commercial advertising doesn't make them marketing specialists—unless they belong to the Direct Marketing Association or the American Advertising Federation. We've seen physicians or engineers in committee meetings attempting to wordsmith advertising copy or critique broadcast commercials instead of leaving it to the professionals who specialize in this line of work. And then they wonder why initiatives fail to produce results!)

Do board members know anything about product promotion? Does the association have a story to tell? How good is the association at getting the message to its members, much less getting awareness in their customer markets? Emulating the competition can have value, but unless you leverage your association's strength in the process, it is more likely to fail than succeed.

Look at the programs, services, products, or activities that you have added in recent years. Do they build on your strength? (This assumes you've taken the time to figure out what your strength is. If you haven't, keep reading. There's a guide for doing so in the next chapter.) When you've marched off into unknown territory, has there been any discussion of how the resources required for this new venture could be better reinvested in the core areas where the association does well? If not, make it a practice to add this discussion when considering new programs and services.

One caution: Sticking to strength requires discipline. And discipline isn't fun—until you realize the paybacks that it can bring. Frankly, returning to your strength over and over can get a little boring. Doing so discourages chasing after new products and services, instead sticking to what you do and know best. It means fighting BSOS (bright shiny object syndrome), which causes people to run after new things. It's a Herculean task to prevent both staff and volunteers from searching the horizon for something new and to make sure they recognize limited capabilities and market realities.

Don't get us wrong. We're not opposed to new programs or services. We believe in value creation. We just know that innovation for innovation's sake leads associations astray and that poorly thought out programs and services can drain an association of resources rather than adding to them. Bottom line: We believe in thoughtful, purposeful, deliberate, and, yes, strategic development rather than the fly-by-the-seat-of-your-pants method of progress we've observed in many associations.

With associations operating in an environment of unprecedented competition, involved volunteers can be very naïve about what it takes to launch a successful new venture. They are apt to sorely underestimate what it takes to shepherd an idea from concept to implementation in today's era of crowded markets and service alternatives. And they talk cavalierly about identifying new sources of net revenue like it was an effortless, uncomplicated walk in the park. They fail to understand that it will likely take a concerted application of the association's most significant strength if they are to have even a chance at success.

Associations' focusing on their strength is more important than ever before for several reasons:

To compete. Few would argue that you can compete effectively from a position of weakness. Competition is intense as associations go head to head with well-funded, carefully crafted for-profit product and service offerings. Though associations aren't, by nature, profit driven, corporations are. They regularly operate from positions of strength, bringing market intelligence, expertise, strategic position, and experience to each new endeavor. These focused, well-heeled, well-staffed companies provide stiff competition for the average association.

It's not just corporations that challenge today's associations. Other associations are a source of relatively new competition. And sometimes an association's own members are competing with the organization for members' time, attention, and money! If your competition is operating from their strength and you aren't, who do you think is at a competitive disadvantage? That's right. You are.

Contrast advanced market research, product development, and marketing expertise with the typical association committee meeting. Colleagues sit around the table, searching for a new "member benefit," brainstorming possibilities. "How about a purchasing group?" suggests one. "Sounds like a good idea to me," says another. The chairperson takes a vote. It passes. And with little thought or direction, no market research, and no consideration about whether the program can ever be self-sustaining, staff is expected to develop a proposal for the next meeting. (Never mind that staff has other obligations—including managing the programs that *do* operate from the association's strength.)

Or consider a board member who comes to a meeting proposing a major public relations initiative to combat claims in the marketplace that are unfavorable to members. Forget that the association is almost exclusively technically oriented and that the staff has little or no experience in public relations, communications, or messaging. And forget that the association may lack funds to adequately combat claims. All in favor say, "Aye." Opposed? Motion carries and off we go. Unfortunately, this is how many association initiatives are undertaken.

To add member value. In kinder, simpler times, associations could add value through new programs, services, and products. And nondues opportunities were plentiful and easy picking. But today, markets are mature and members have more options than they can even consider. The internet has been a game changer.

Today's members are savvy, informed, and discerning consumers. Adding value requires associations to think differently, playing to their strength like never before. Associations need disciplined focus that allows them to meaningfully compete. Performance will result from consciously understanding and capitalizing on the things the association does exceptionally well. Where you have human capital or intellectual property that has high value in the marketplace. Where you have a unique position. Where you perform better than anyone else. Where you have a corner on the market. Where you have a strong partnership that provides exclusive expertise. Where you have well-developed, proven marketing abilities.

The market will be unkind to you if you don't optimize your strength (Maybe you're already seeing this in some aspect of your work.) To thrive in today's climate, your association's most valuable assets must be fully utilized.

To respond to the "do more with less" challenge. As the ability to raise dues is diminished and as increasingly competitive markets for nondues services crimps net revenue generation, the importance of capitalizing on previously underoptimized organizational strength becomes apparent. Let's say an association's once dominant annual meeting encounters blistering competition from specialty associations, for-profit providers, and members themselves. Can the association continue its course of diversifying into new, uncharted service areas or does it need to increase resource allocations and focus its energy to what it does best? Or say a professional society has the ability to attract the best expertise in the field. Can it allow this intellectual capital to flounder on a committee with an ill-defined charge, or should it mobilize the expertise to produce something of value in a more efficient task force model?

The association of the future can ill afford to let its strength sit idle. A basketball team cannot leave its highest scoring player on the bench. The more the high performer is on the court, the more successful the team will be. The same is true for associations. The demands of a competitive marketplace require that strength be leveraged to create more strength. As iron sharpens iron, associations operating from strength create more strength. And the more strength the association displays, the more membership becomes something of value in the marketplace and a "must have" for your members.

To compete, you must begin by assessing your strength. Most associations fall short in this area. There are many ways to discover your strength. We'll cover them in the next chapter.

CHAPTER THREE

Assessing Strengths

> *"The point here is not that you should always forgo...*
> *weakness fixing. The point is that you should see it*
> *for what it is: damage control, not development. And*
> *as we mentioned earlier, damage control can prevent*
> *failure, but it will never elevate you to excellence."*
> —MARCUS BUCKINGHAM[9]

Most associations think they are building on their strength. A closer look reveals that even if they are, they often leave a lot on the sidelines.

The analysis of strength is often superficial. As consultants, we're guilty of developing lists of some very loosely defined "strengths" in strategic planning sessions, mostly in the interest of time. (To attempt to overcome this, we require associations to force rank their strengths to improve the identification of the most significant.) Overall, associations need to dig deeper. Associations must guard against what tends to be the politically correct strength, like "our people!" What people? Members? Leadership? Staff? What about them? What is it they do well? What expertise do they have? An in-depth, introspective analysis is required. It needs to be objective, candid, and thorough. Good questions, like the following, can help. They may not produce perfectly clear answers, but they are a starting point.

(Note that they are from an external perspective to give you some distance from internal biases.)

- What would our competitors say we do exceptionally well?
- Where are we dominant in the marketplace? Where do we have high market share?
- Where have others attempted to compete with us and failed?
- If we asked members to play "word association" with us, when we say the "XYZ Association" what word or phrase would come immediately to mind?
- If we asked members to identify the one thing that we do that helps them most, what would they say?
- What are we not doing that we should be doing that expands on existing strength?

Don't allow your association to operate on "pseudo strength." Make sure your strength is real. Association staff and volunteers often believe that their programs, services, or activities are better than they really are. While there is nothing wrong with believing in the association, be careful not to "drink the Kool-Aid." Real strength has value in the marketplace. Real strength results in something people will invest time and money in. Bottom line: People pay (in other words, write a dues check) to gain access to real strength.

Sometimes strength is an association program or service that adds considerable value or excels in the marketplace. Strengths can also be underlying capabilities that are used to develop or deliver an association's value proposition. Still other strengths are critical in the association's positioning, communications, marketing, or relationships. This is another way to analyze strength:

- What programs, services, or other deliverables are of particular value to our members?
- What systems, processes, or operational aspects of the association are essential to delivering value?

• What are the association's strengths in relation to its communications, positioning, marketing, or relationships?

In addition to often being superficial, the assessment of an association's strength is often incomplete. Every association needs a comprehensive catalogue of its strengths, assets, resources, and capital, even if some are intangible and difficult to quantify.

Another way to identify and evaluate your association's strengths is to organize them into four "buckets." While definitions vary and there will be overlap, relax! This is simply an exercise to help you dig deeper into the analysis. The four "buckets" are assets, resources, capabilities, and intangibles.

Assets. For our purposes, we will define an asset as an "item of ownership having value." The first asset that comes to mind is an association's headquarters facility. Is our building a strength and are we fully leveraging it? For example, the Colorado Automobile Dealers Association (CADA) gains a lot of mileage from their headquarters building, using it for receptions, press conferences, banquets, and meetings with dealers, legislators, charitable organizations, other associations, the media, and the public. CADA President Tim Jackson, CMP, CAE, says, "The association facility was designed to leverage its potential for convening meetings, forums, and receptions. The building is in constant use. Hardly a day goes by without one or more catered functions. I'd estimate that we host some kind of meeting or event four out of five days in an average week." The receptions provide the association with valuable face time with legislators and regulators. The meetings connect the association with the members. The forums build relationships with the media and other centers of influence.

The Texas Trial Lawyers Association capitalized on property it owned adjacent to the Texas State Capitol by building a six-story headquarters there in 2000. A kitchen and dining area is used for lunches and receptions daily when the legislature is in session. Members and legislators have an opportunity for critical interaction in an informal setting. The association has a unique occasion to articulate its positions and increase its influence. The building also produces revenue, as TTLA occupies two floors and rents out the rest at premium rates.

The Metro Denver Dental Society plans to stake its claim in the continuing education arena by building a regional education center that houses not only its headquarters office but includes advanced technology and on-site operatories for hands-on clinical education for dentists. According to Elizabeth Price, CAE, executive director, the society will partner with area study clubs and well-established education providers to make the concept a reality and will also offer the facility to large conventions. And, notes Price, when not being used for continuing education, the facility "will be used by our Metro Denver Dental Foundation (MDDF) to serve patients through the Smile Again Program and other future programs."

While these associations are maximizing use of their largest assets, more than a few associations have physical assets that are underused—empty classrooms, empty office space, and elaborate boardrooms that are used three times a year.

Another common association asset is a trade show or major annual conference. These are usually profitable enterprises, and most associations use the net revenue they generate to subsidize a wide range of programs and services. Associations and professional societies need to exercise care here. Excessive "milking" of these assets to support other programs and services has a downside: The failure to continually reinvest in the trade show or annual conference can lead to a loss of competitive position, prestige, or perception. Make sure that your "cash cow" has plenty of hay to graze on before you start spreading it around to other activities!

One should ask: If the programs and services we are subsidizing are so valuable, why do we need to subsidize them? Why can't we charge enough for them to recover our costs? Are we squandering resources propping up marginal services when those resources would be better reinvested in our profitable, competitive trade show or conference?

Other common assets are brands, trademarks, training programs, proven curriculums, and member/non-member mailing lists, to name a few. Bottom line: Are you adequately using your assets on behalf of the association and your members? For example, are you treating your member database like an important and unique asset? Are your competitors saying, "I wish we had that (insert building, member database, conference, etc.). They don't appreciate what they have. We could make a killing if we had that!"

Resources are a source of supply, support, or aid, especially one that can be readily drawn upon when needed.

An association's volunteer base is often, and legitimately, identified as a strength. A trade association often has access to industry leaders. Professional societies often attract the best in the profession. This is a considerable potential resource, but it is often suboptimized.

How many millions of hours do company presidents or executives collectively sit in unproductive association board meetings each year? How many hundreds of hours do professional experts idle in fruitless society committee meetings annually? If you paid your association's board, committee, and task force volunteers the market rate for their time, how much would it be? And what kind of return are you getting from this substantial resource?

Increasing time pressures and higher expectations for return on investment of time will make tapping this resource even more challenging in the future. A common reason for rejecting an invitation to serve on a board is, "I don't have the time." Executives and professionals have considerable demands on their time at work and in their personal lives. They have 24 hours a day, and they are scrutinizing how they spend their time like they never have before. They are unlikely to spin their wheels in unproductive board or committee meetings that don't efficiently tap their input or expertise. Further, as workforce downsizing continues at member companies and the workload increases for your members, it gets harder and harder for members to justify their involvement in your organization and/or absence from their respective companies.

Another time-related consequence for associations is that senior-level executives who have the authority to make decisions on behalf of their companies are less able to find the time to serve on an association board, instead pushing the responsibility to midlevel managers. These executives often aren't able to pledge or commit resources to the association without checking in with headquarters or first having to convince higher-ups, which can slow projects, momentum, and support for the association.

Service on boards and participation on committees have been the traditional means to tap the human capital of the volunteer base. But serving as a director on what is typically a large, rubber-stamp board has limited value to busy executives and professionals. And you have to ask yourself: If we could somehow measure the collective value of the human capital of our board of directors, what percentage of that resource are we tapping today? When asked this question, audiences of volunteer leaders and association executives often reply, "Less than 20 percent." Quite an indictment of the system.

Serving on a committee for several years may likewise have limited appeal today and in the future. How many committees really produce results? And do business executives and professionals have the time and interest to participate in unproductive activity?

We are convinced that the primary model for mobilizing the volunteer resource is the project-specific, time-limited task force or work group. We also like the terms "quick action teams" or "strike forces." In this case, the volunteers know exactly what the assignment is. They know exactly what time commitment is involved. They know that the task force or work group will be well focused. Associations have been moving toward this model for years, but they still cling more to committees than task forces when it should be the other way around. One of our clients has more than 100 committees! Want to bet how many of them make use of the resources available and produce something of value?

Eliminate all committees other than those that meet the following criteria: (1) require volunteer expertise or oversight and (2) recur annually. Period. Every other initiative requiring volunteers should go the task force or work group route.

Consider the AMC Institute, the trade association for association management companies. These organizations run thousands of associations. They work extensively with association volunteers. Does the AMC Institute have committees? No. They rely exclusively on task forces for activating their members and do so with great results.

When it comes to the human capital of staff, this resource is also often underoptimized in the current association model. Just recall a recent meeting when your board or committee went on at length in discussion of an issue. Staff sat quietly on the sidelines, knowing that it was expected that they not contribute to the conversation. It is likely that the staff had significantly more knowledge of the issue and more insight regarding how it might be resolved than anyone in the room. This is the classic example of not building on strength in human resources. But it is only the tip of the iceberg.

In addition to staff opinions not being solicited or incorporated into decision making, the staff resource is squandered in a myriad of ways. High-potential staff doing administrative work. Hand-holding volunteers. Chasing well-intentioned but half-baked proposals down rabbit holes. Boards are quick to identify staff as a significant strength and twice as quick to fritter away this resource by not creating a true partnership.

The other resource that associations are likely to identify is their financial position or reserves. While some will identify strong sources of net revenue, they are more likely to point to their healthy reserve position. This is unquestionably a source of support that can be readily drawn upon when needed. The only problem for most associations is that nobody knows when they should draw on reserves, which negates their value as an organizational strength.

We would contend that it is difficult to consider a resource a strength when you can't or won't use it. Consider what Steve Gennett, former CEO of Carolinas Associated General Contractors, Inc., said: "I think associations overplay the reserve dollars in terms of funding that has to be built up and maintained. I have been in this business for 43 years. I can't even count on three fingers the number of times that we had a significant stress in the operation where we had to say, 'Well, we've got reserves to back this up.'"[10]

In our opinion, association reserves are an underused resource. In fact, a fundamental difference between corporations and associations is financial strategy. While most corporations leverage their financial position with debt, associations do just the opposite and hoard cash. We don't understand it.

In a recent strategy session, the leadership of the Atlanta Apartment Association agreed that investing in their technology platform was far more important than contributing to reserves. In fact, they agreed that, at least in the short term, reserves could be purposely drawn down to fund technology capacity building. And, as we wrote about in *Race for Relevance,* Carolinas Associated General Contractors, Inc. funded—with reserves—the development of bidding software that eventually produced revenue of $1.6 million per year![11]

Capabilities. For this analysis, we would consider capabilities as qualities, abilities, and aptitudes that can be used or developed. Identifying capabilities may take a little digging. What is it that your association is really good at? In what aspect of your organization do you regularly execute better than any other? Where do you perform well in a way that differentiates yours from other organizations?

The Personal Care Products Council has a public affairs committee that has been effective in responding to attacks on industry practices by activists deftly using social media. They are able to respond with urgency, effectively using the association's scientific research to counter activist claims. This rapid response capability is a major strength.

In a strategic planning session, the Michigan Association of CPAs conducted an in-depth analysis of their most valuable capabilities. After much discussion and introspection, they concluded that they are really good at managing projects. Regardless of the challenge or objective, they are good at organizing and managing the necessary processes to get the job done. This project management capability is a key association strength because it translates into the ability to clearly define what's challenging members, create a project to address it, and implement a plan that results in member value.

Intangibles. By definition, these are things incapable of being perceived by the sense of touch. Think about your association's *brand.* Many association brands are well recognized. And in most cases they convey a positive image. If this is the case, does your association really get all the mileage it can from its brand identity? Is it ubiquitous in everything you do, deliver, and communicate? Is it well curated? Is there consistency in its promotion and development?

We have come across more than one national association with affiliates in which the affiliates do not brand themselves consistently with the national organization. What are they thinking? What has more value, one strong nationally recognized brand or 23 different identities for fundamentally the same organization?

Community is another common association intangible. Members in an industry or profession have an affinity for their association. Does your association capitalize on this sense of belonging? Does it capitalize on collegiality? Does it recognize the power of bringing members together to commiserate, discuss challenges, and solve problems? (Note: Affinity alone is not sufficient in an environment where competition trumps loyalty and and from our perspective, member expectations are becoming increasingly important versus "for the good of the order.")

An association's *momentum* can be a significant resource. When membership is increasing, attendance is growing, and use of new services exceeds expectations, the association has the potential to capitalize on momentum. Momentum can be a powerful tool, giving a tailwind to new initiatives and reducing risks. Momentum also helps build trust, as partners see each other's capabilities and begin to rely on one another, and can open previously closed doors.

In a two-day strategy retreat we facilitated, participants agreed on a set of the association's key strengths. On the second day, a participant commented, "We missed our most significant strength. If you look at our performance in recent years, our progress has been substantial. We are able to do things today that were impossible not so long ago. And our potential going forward is considerable. Our biggest strength is our momentum!" No one disagreed. Yet intangible strengths are often overlooked. The lesson? Don't neglect your intangibles. They are often significant.

An association's *position* often can be valuable. It may simply be a high profile in the industry or profession or it may be its unique ability to add value because of developments in the industry or field. Examples include an association with a position as an advocate in an environment where legislative proposals unfavorable to the industry are accelerating or an association with a strong science and research position in a field where loosely based negative claims are being made in the marketplace.

Reputation is another intangible. Does your association's reputation help you address emerging issues proactively and positively? Does it open doors for you with regulators and legislators? Does it allow you to convene industry meetings with all players present? Many associations have been around a long time and have been consistent and reliable, making them trusted partners. Reputation often translates into being able to get things done quickly and effectively.

They say *knowledge* is power. What's in your association's knowledge bank? Are you tapping it for the benefit of the industry or profession you serve? Are you capitalizing on and mobilizing this knowledge? Both individuals and associations tend to undervalue their knowledge, assuming that everyone else knows what they know. This is simply not true. Knowledge may be one of the most valuable intangibles.

The four buckets outlined above provide an effective method for identifying and assessing your strengths. Sometimes this exercise alone will be eye-opening. If you're not able to list your strengths, that's instructive in itself. And if you are able to articulate multiple strengths, there is value in ranking them for future decision-making purposes.

Core Business

Since real strength is often difficult to identify, we're including a couple of ways, other than the "buckets," to identify it. Some refer to strength as your "core business" or "core competency."

In his book, *Profit from the Core*, Chris Zook defines a core business as "the set of products, capabilities, customers, channels, and geographies that defines the essence of what the company [read: association] is or aspires to be."[12]

Zook's concept of a "set" is particularly applicable to associations. The typical association model is just that: a set of programs and services, member markets, distribution, and geographic scope. But the traditional association set can be a mismatch with the current environment. Association programs and services tend to be less competitive than they once were. Capabilities have to be effectively leveraged for performance, and many associations fall short here.

To identify your association's core business, ask yourself the following questions:

• Who are our most active and most important members?
• What do we do better than anyone else?

- What do we do that differentiates our association from competitors?
- What association programs, services, or activities are critical to our members?
- What do we do that members can't do for themselves—and that they don't get without being a member?
- What are our most important delivery channels?
- What other association assets or resources contribute to the above?
- What is running smoothly and working well in the association?
- Where are we under-resourced; where don't we have enough support either financially or from a human resource standpoint? (Asking this question will help eliminate items that you might otherwise include on your list of core strengths.)

An analysis of the answers to these questions will give you some valuable insights into your association's core business.

Core Competency

Whether you call it a strength, core business, or core competency (as do C.K. Prahalad and Gary Hamel in their 1990 article, "The Core Competence of the Corporation"), competencies are developed over time and are critical to competitive position. This idea is important to understand in the context of increased competition in the association arena. As we look for strengths, we must pay careful attention to those that give us an edge.

Hamel and Prahalad's criteria for a core competence provide yet another evaluation scheme for association volunteers and executives in analyzing and building on strength. Their three criteria for a competence to be "core" are:

1. It is very difficult for competitors to copy.
2. It can be used for multiple products or in multiple markets.
3. It must contribute to the end user's experienced value.[13]

Today, most association programs and services are easily duplicated. Name one service that your association offers that is not available elsewhere. We think this will be a short list. Speed and continuous innovation are keys to staying ahead of competitors, but associations are not particularly adept at either because of resource limitations and/or dependence on a lengthy volunteer approval process. Success for associations will come from more effectively tapping the association's member and staff intellectual capital to create improved competitive advantage and speed up the approval process. (Note: If your association operates with a House of Delegates, essentially you are able to move the association's business ahead only once a year—unless you are lucky enough to be one of the few that allows the board to operate aggressively in between delegate assembly meetings.)

A competency is not a product or a service. It is an underlying capability that has value in multiple programs, services, or markets. One school of thought is that the primary core competency of an association is the ability to use the member base. The membership base can be mobilized for grassroots lobbying activity, leveraged for its expertise through committees or task forces, or tapped as a market for educational offerings. The membership provides a base from which to fundraise. In essence, the association's ability to bring people together and employ the community's strength in numbers toward whatever aims can be seen as a core competency.

There's also the value question. What is it that you have that really adds value? Association leaders can have exaggerated opinions of what has value. But only the members and the marketplace actually determine what has value. Look at participation levels and what's selling to determine where your value is. Refer to member survey results to identify why members join and stay. These specifics help identify your value.

The Hedgehog Concept

One final source for assessing strengths comes from Jim Collin's book *Good to Great*. In it, he introduces the hedgehog concept, so named because the hedgehog "knows one big thing" and "reduces all challenges and dilemmas to simple—indeed almost simplistic—hedgehog ideas." [14] Consequently, the hedgehog concept is "a simple, crystalline concept that flows from deep understanding about the intersection"[15] of the following:

1. Does the association have a deep and passionate commitment to this product, service, or market?

2. Is the association the best in the world at producing it?

3. Does it drive the association's economic engine?

Association members, volunteers, and staff are often deeply passionate about the industry or profession they serve. This can be a unique resource that competitors lack. But passion alone won't cut it today. Associations are full of people who have passion for the organization but don't perform. Passion must result in value creation for members or strengthen the association's ability to deliver that value.

Best in class? Far too much of what associations offer today is run of the mill. What deliverable do you offer that is the best in the world? This is an important question and a considerable challenge, particularly for the small association.

Driving the economic engine is probably the easiest of the hedgehog concepts for associations to address. The average association can eliminate 80 to 90 percent of what it does from hedgehog consideration because these products, services, and activities are not its economic engine. In general, associations subsidize far too much of what they offer. Concentrating resources on your economic engines and reinvesting in them is a critical strategy for associations. The economic engine test guards against identifying pseudo strengths. The market validates strength with its pocketbook. Revenue and dues follow value. And revenue creates options and opportunities for associations.

The Weakness or Problem Trap

Instead of focusing on strengths, why not fix weaknesses? Why not solve problems? It is difficult to argue with the need to correct short-comings or remedy a concern. One could easily make the case that to be a world-class organization, we should strive for robust excellence, bolstering areas that are weak and aggressively tackling problems.

Yet problem solving and fixes simply get you back to normal. They don't really advance the association toward its goals or objectives. And in the final analysis, are fundamental weaknesses ever really fixed? Many problems confronting a profession or industry are beyond the ability of an association to solve, yet association leaders often dive in under member pressure without honestly assessing what thinly spreading precious financial and human capital will mean. While no organization can ignore weaknesses or problems, particularly if they are widespread and debilitating, the time and energy is often more productive when allocated to strengths. Mitigate the weaknesses; build on the strengths.

Think of a typical grade school student. He may gravitate to math or science or be more attracted to the arts or humanities. He will perform better in one or the other. What do teachers and parents do? They focus on the weakness, prescribing additional or remedial work. However, research by author Marcus Buckingham shows that time would be better spent on where students have interests and aptitudes, challenging and encouraging students according to their natural strengths. Buckingham says, "You can see this amplification process most clearly when it comes to your strengths. Your strengths are a multiplier. Invest time and energy and training in them and you will get an exponential return."[16] This applies to associations as well. Strengths are multipliers.

When you work to strengthen a strength, as Jean Van Rensselar writes, "You'll be 'majoring on your majors' and 'minoring on your minors.'"[17] In the long run, focusing on strength is a powerful strategy, especially when dealing with limited human and financial resources.

Finally, notes Chris Zook in *Profit from the Core*, "We have found that when most management teams seek to revitalize the growth of a company, they focus on the underperforming business units. We argue that growth requires focusing instead on increasing the performance of the best business, no matter how well they are doing at the present. The best business is in the best position to deliver better growth."[18] The same is true for associations.

The Optimum Scenario: Strength Matched with Opportunity

Now that you've defined your strengths, it's time to rigorously refine and reduce the list to one or two that you can fully exploit as a matter of priority.

The optimum scenario is when your association's environment presents you with an opportunity that is the perfect match to your core strength. This assumes that you have a process for scanning the marketplace and staying on top of developments that have consequences for members, in particular, searching for high-impact trends that require changes in the way companies operate or professionals practice.

An association with a strong educational position has an immediate opportunity when a new regulation is instituted. Members need to know how to comply efficiently to minimize the potentially negative costs or stress implications, such as a CPA society's addressing changes in the tax law or a manufacturing trade association's explaining a new environmental regulation.

Certification represents another area of potential in codifying the necessary knowledge base for members at various career stages. For example, education has been a top priority for the California Association of Community Managers, Inc. (CACM) since its inception. Over the years its educational offerings have become the association's greatest strength. At the time of CACM's formation, there were no established core competencies or standards of practice within the California common interest development (CID) industry. CACM paved the way for professional community management standards by creating programs, events, conferences, and courses centered on industry education.

CACM also established the Certified Community Association Manager (CCAM) designation, which has grown into the mark of professional achievement recognized by the state of California. As the industry evolved, CACM identified a need for advanced coursework and an advanced level of certification. This need sparked a five-year process of research and development as the association worked to create several key advanced education and certification programs. Early in the process, CACM's research demonstrated that not all community managers may be ready to pursue a master level of achievement once their CCAM had been attained. This insight spawned the simultaneous creation of a Specialty Certificate Program, which now awards certificates in high rise, large scale, portfolio, and active adult community management, with plans to include a certificate in homebuilder communities in the near future. The first certificates were awarded in 2011, the same year the association's Master of Community Association Management (MCAM) certification debuted. These certification programs are now being introduced in other states, with similar associations replicating the CACM model.

In another example of focusing on strength, the Minneapolis Area Association of Realtors® (MAAR) realized it was sitting on a gold mine in the form of its Multiple Listing Service (MLS) data. Using rich, detailed, and current information, the association began assembling practical, meaningful, and perhaps most important, local metrics such as new listings, closed sales, and days on market. An immediate hit, the simplified reports led to a foreclosure report, one-page "hyper local" reports for individual suburbs and city neighborhoods, and a more robust and visually pleasing annual report for the entire Minneapolis-Saint Paul metropolitan area. The idea was stunningly simple.

Word spread and so did demand for the reports. MAAR formed a company within the association, called 10K Research and Marketing, that partners with Realtor® associations, MLS organizations, brokers, and other real estate companies across North America to create visually compelling reports, interactive tools, videos, and infographics. Seven of the association's 24 staff members are dedicated to 10K Research operations and others are regularly involved in aspects of marketing and managing the internal group.

In less than four years, 10K has gone from pulling data from just one MLS to more than 150 MLSs and now provides market trends products to more than 250 strategic partners. We love how 10K Research describes itself: *We provide the knowledge that an egghead values and the "aha!" that a consumer needs.*

Matching Strength with Opportunity

A simple matrix can be helpful when matching your strength with opportunity:

High-Impact Trends	Association Strength #1: _____	Association Strength #2: _____	Association Strength #3: _____

List the strengths across the top and the high-impact environmental trends in the vertical column. For each trend, indicate the degree (high, medium, or low) that the association's strength can be brought to bear on the trend. Focus on the areas where your association has a high degree of capitalizing on strength.

Does Sticking with Strength Stifle Innovation?

There has been much discussion about the value and importance of innovation in the association community. If an association disciplines itself to focus on its strength, won't that limit its ability to innovate?

First, we need to be clear about what innovation is. Many confuse it with creativity or developing new ideas. While innovation does involve creativity and ideas, it entails much more. There is a long road from an idea to an innovation.

In *Management: Tasks, Responsibilities and Practices,* Peter Drucker stated, "Only after a new product or a new business has been established in the market is there an 'innovation.' It is by now accepted, if only as a rule of thumb, that for every dollar spent on generating an idea, ten dollars have to be spent on 'research' to convert it into a new discovery or a new invention. For every ten dollars spent on 'research,' at least one hundred dollars need to be spent on development, and for every hundred dollars spent on development, something between a thousand and ten thousand dollars are needed to introduce and establish a new product or a new business on the market." [19]

The Indiana Dental Association's (IDA) editorial board is in the innovation game, creating a "new business" in an old arena: continuing education (CE). Working with the editorial board, Will Sears, director of communications, took a proactive role and came up with a creative idea: a self-study continuing education book featuring a variety of topics appealing to dentists and hygienists alike. The book, *Foundations,* will be produced via an online fulfillment service and enables participants to submit their responses through a specially designed section of the IDA website. Upon completion of the program, participants receive their CE certificates automatically via email.

In Indiana, dentists must complete 20 hours of continuing education annually, with at least 10 coming from live training. The new book and online submission component will provide a solid option for completing the nonlive portion of this requirement. At just $20 per credit hour, it's extremely affordable and participants never have to leave their offices.

To keep production costs down, Sears reached out to the IDA membership for help recruiting nationally known speakers and authors in dentistry who were willing to donate expert submissions for the book. Next, he used the IDA's own website committee to oversee the upgraded functionality of the website.

At press time, initial sales had surpassed $16,200. This could easily increase as IDA opens up space for online advertising as well as a profit-sharing model with other state dental societies that choose to promote the resource to their members.

The average association doesn't have the financial resources to be truly innovative unless it is willing to use reserves as a research and development fund in addition to as a rainy day fund. This is a radical change in thinking for most association boards that have been schooled to hoard reserve funds "just in case." For some associations, the need to make tardy technology upgrades and advances is so great that the rainy day has arrived. For others, rapid declines in both membership and revenues mean that the day has come to use reserves to offset deficits. Though we agree that reserves should be used wisely, we've seen too many associations refuse to use them at all, creating a cash stash that benefits the association's financial position more than it does the association's members.

Now that we have clarified innovation, let's think about the prospects for any innovation that doesn't build on an association's strengths. Innovation is very difficult, particularly in mature markets. Only one in 10 attempts is likely to be successful, and maybe even less than that. Because of these odds, we believe the only intelligent course is to innovate based on strengths.

What about Challenges or Opportunities Without Strength?

What does an association do when confronted with a situation where it is not equipped with necessary organizational capabilities or resources? What does the association do when an opportunity or challenge presents itself and the organizational strength required is absent?

The current imperative for associations to adopt technology is a good example. For most associations, technology is not a strength. Many are still focused on face-to-face and print-centric communication though the emerging technology opportunities are digital and internet-based. In today's environment, the question becomes, "How can we use technology to further strengthen our strength?"

If a society has a strong continuing education and professional development menu of traditional seminars, conferences, and workshops, it should focus on this strength. It should leverage its position as a respected source of education and the quality of its content in making the transition to webinars and other e-learning delivery channels. It should capitalize on the expertise present at its continuing education programs and trade show by recording, repurposing, archiving, and making the materials available after the conference—either for sale or as part of member benefits.

Overall, a strategy of focusing on strength, rather than lamenting weakness, creates a more powerful position for your association. Further, it can be both motivating and energizing for volunteers and staff alike, since nothing breeds success like success. People want to be involved with organizations that have energy and vitality.

The Role of the CEO

The opportunities and challenges in the marketplace will not always line up with your association's strength. It's a dilemma when this happens. The knee-jerk reaction is to panic and focus on getting stronger in your weak areas. But it's often possible to find a way to focus on the situation or issue in a way that works to your advantage. This requires a commitment to stepping back and taking a look at the broader picture rather than focusing too narrowly on only one aspect. While some volunteer leaders are able to do this, many are not. In this case, staff can provide valuable guidance and an important perspective.

Building on strength sounds easy, but it is challenging in practice. It requires rigorous analysis. It requires time. It requires creative deployment. It requires honesty. Large boards that are not composed for performance likely will struggle with these requirements. Boards that do not empower their CEO will also struggle to develop and consider the results of an honest assessment.

Don't underestimate what a strength analysis takes. In *Good to Great*, Collins notes that it took four years for some of the companies he studied to clarify their hedgehog concept.[20] How many boards do you know that would commit to this degree of introspection and analysis? We don't know of any. And if even they did, board turnover means the exercise will eventually be forgotten. However, the empowered CEO takes ownership of the process and serves as the board's institutional memory. The CEO must be the association's steward of strategy.

Once strengths are identified, the work starts. Discipline is required. Creative approaches must be applied. The typical board, as most are currently constituted, is not necessarily skilled in these areas. The traditional board meeting is focused on reporting on activities since the last board meeting, not on looking ahead to the future. It's focused on motions, debate, and votes to provide direction to various committees, task forces, and staff, not on an in-depth discussion of trends or challenges. It is focused on the order imposed by parliamentary procedure, not the chaos and discomfort sometimes necessary for an organization to innovate or move to a new level.

We're not opposed to orderly board meetings, but we do advocate for providing discussion time that isn't linked to motions and votes. Exploration time is important to fully understanding issues, providing input, and coming to consensus on future strategy and plans.

Many associations are governed by large boards with directors based on geography, special interests, who they know, or tenure in the industry rather than by competency-based boards in which carefully selected individuals are elected or appointed based on their skills, talents, and abilities. It's difficult to tackle the in-depth analysis needed to discover strengths or core competencies when directors don't naturally possess these skills or when tradition dictates a more formal approach to governance.

Until associations embrace a small, competency-based board as we proposed in *Race for Relevance,* performance in building on strength will be heavily dependent on the CEO. The CEO committed to this strategy will yield results and keep the board on track. The CEO will commit the time (perhaps years) to digging to the core of the association's strength. The CEO will bring discipline to exploiting the strength and deflecting efforts to wander off in different directions. The CEO will understand that relevance is required in the new normal for associations and that focusing on strength is an important point on the road to relevance for members.

The Role of the Board

If you're a volunteer association leader, you can help your staff and CEO with your willingness to dig deeply enough to identify strengths and your commitment to focusing on them. You can help by avoiding BSOS (bright shiny object syndrome) and talking other leaders out of it when you see them begin to wander. You can commit to the discipline of remaining focused rather than trying to be all things to all people by adding poorly considered programs and services. (Consider that Jack Welch, retired CEO of General Electric, had only four different number-one priorities during the 20 years he led the company and that Bill Gates built Microsoft based on a simple vision: a computer on every desk and in every home. That's focus!) You can personally measure ideas against the strategic plan (Your association does have one, right?) and encourage abandoning ideas that don't match up. And you can speak up and vocally support any efforts to capitalize on strength.

Strategies for Success

Part of the value of focusing on strengths is that doing so gives you permission to say no to things that rest outside your area of strongest influence. This is hard for many associations because of the complexity of "keeping members happy" and juggling multiple constituencies. But don't underestimate the power that comes with a clear value proposition and knowing who you are as an association. The following strategies for success will help you gain this power and clarity:

- Complete a thorough, in-depth analysis of core strength.
- Fully exploit your association's strength.
- Stick to your core strength and refuse to be diverted.
- Recognize that addressing weaknesses can improve performance but meaningful success comes from innovating from strength.
- Acknowledge that sometimes it's best to solve a problem not by focusing on it but by creating a success elsewhere.

- Reinvest in strength to increase the likelihood of a greater return on investment.
- Understand that your greatest potential for growth comes from what you are already good at.

Building on strength is a cornerstone of strategy. This is fundamental, as you will see in the coming chapters. Capitalizing on your association's strength is foundational to the remaining strategies of concentrating resources, integrating programs and services for good fit, aligning people and processes for lean operations, and abandoning programs purposefully when necessary. Start with strength. Then, and only then, are you ready to proceed to the next chapter.

Case Study

Focus on Standards Drives Global Strategy

ASSOCIATION: IPC—Association Connecting Electronics Industries

BUDGET: $15,000,000

NUMBER OF STAFF MEMBERS: 108 FTE

NUMBER OF MEMBERS: 3,300

Though it's been a decade since IPC identified globalization as a strategy for the association, one thing hasn't changed. From the beginning, the association recognized the value of focusing on its strength in standard setting as the ticket to take IPC to other parts of the world and grow the organization's influence outside of the United States.

A three-year grant from the U.S. Department of Commerce to help associations expand standardization activity in China allowed IPC to open an office in Shanghai in 2002. China was the first step for the association, since it is one of the largest manufacturing bases in the world. At the time, there was little information about starting overseas endeavors and IPC learned—through experience—that the traditional membership model (You pay dues; you become a member; you get benefits.) didn't work as well in China as in the United States. Instead, the association learned to lead with service rather than membership, raising awareness of both IPC standards and the training provided to understand them.

Through trial and error, IPC has developed a three-step process for entering new markets. First, the association provides technically accurate translations of its standards. When entering China, says David Bergman, vice president for international relations, "We didn't want to just translate the words. We wanted to translate the meaning and the only way to do that is with a committee to debate what it means and ask a lot of questions. If it's not clear in English, you're not going to make it clear in Chinese."

Once the standard translation is complete, the committee carefully reviews the standard. This naturally develops standards experts who are familiar with the document and are able to help review and revise the standard every five years in accordance with the American National Standards Institute's requirements. The third step is new standards development, which is also handled by committee. Though many associations have to pay committee members, IPC has 35 technical committees in China, all composed of unpaid volunteers and committee leaders.

Experience in China has helped global expansion elsewhere. The association now has one representative in Europe, one in Russia, and 10 staff in India. Bergman says, "We learned a lot about approaching a new market, so it's going faster. After two years, China had two staff. After two years in India, we have 10 staff. We've learned a few lessons." These lessons reinforce leading from strength by remaining focused on standard setting and standards training as IPC enters new markets.

Though India is moving more quickly, the potential in China remains enormous. After 10 years, IPC now has a staff of 36 spread across eight Chinese cities, and membership increased 35 percent between 2010 and 2011. The growth is strong enough that the association plans to hire a president for IPC China.

The training model abroad differs from that in the United States. Stateside, licensed training centers pay IPC a franchise fee to offer certification. According to Bergman, "In China and India we do it with staff. This gives us a member service so we can create a member/nonmember rate. It also allows us to get closer to the customers to understand what challenges they might be having and to help them build awareness for our standards."

Flexibility is key when expanding globally. Now that IPC is established in China, the association is considering more traditional member services such as lobbying and tradeshows. Even with new service offerings, IPC remains focused in the standards arena in its work abroad.

Though many associations will never venture overseas, the IPC lesson is this: Lead from your strength. IPC knows its muscle is standard setting and it's used that as a calling card as the association meets the globalization goal it set a decade ago. Strength is a multiplier. When you lead from your strength, you win.

Case Study

Leading with Learning

ASSOCIATION: Society of Manufacturing Engineers

BUDGET: 40 Million

NUMBER OF STAFF MEMBERS: 185

NUMBER OF MEMBERS: 24,000

Though face-to-face education has always been a strength for the Society of Manufacturing Engineers (SME), the organization reached a point where it had knowledge customers wanted but wasn't delivering it in the way learners wanted to receive it (online). It's a disconnect facing a growing number of associations.

Based on this knowledge, the association identified becoming a "premier provider for manufacturing knowledge" as a strategic planning goal. As a result, SME restructured the professional development department by incorporating certification into the area, more fully allowing the body of knowledge for certification to become the driver for the knowledge provided to the industry. As a result, certification is growing.

According to Mark Tomlinson, CEO, SME was able to meet this goal more rapidly by choosing an aggressive route. He notes, "There's incrementalism, where you just continually try to grow your own existing products organically. Or you can make a step change, and what we decided was that we needed to make a step change if we truly wanted to be relevant in this space."

Step change (versus incrementalism) as a strategy is overlooked by most associations. Instead of creating premier education from the inside out, SME worked from the outside in by buying Tooling U, a company created specifically to support manufacturing related learning. According to Tomlinson, "We improved our time to market by years by purchasing versus making, and we can improve the quality based on existing product rather than having to do quality checks on developing a product."

The bold move paid off. Though the purchase was a significant investment for SME from its reserves, the association expects double digit growth per year—so far growth is exceeding the projections in the second year—and an expected payback time of seven years. Also important is the fact that the association is realizing its goal of becoming a premier knowledge provider for manufacturing.

Not every association is positioned for or has the support of the board for such large initiatives. Tomlinson provides some historical perspective that's helpful for association executives and volunteer leaders:

> "The board recognized seven years ago that it had to refocus its energies away from being just representative of the membership base and be more representative of the industry that we're serving. They made a commitment to downsize the board from 30 to 14. Based on a smaller board, with a more rigorous selection process for board candidates, we now have a board that is pushing us to think strategically and allows me to work with the board in regard to strategic thinking as well."

Today, the nominating committee aggressively scans the landscape for the right people to add to the board of directors and interviews the candidates who apply. Says Tomlinson, "It used to be membership activities and loyalty to the membership that got you a board position. Now it's more your ability to articulate strategies based on your expertise and experience in the manufacturing industry."

With board support, acquisition is now an active strategy for SME. Though it started prior to the purchase of Tooling U with the addition of several trade shows in Canada, it's now a planned activity with a committee assigned to look at mergers and acquisitions as a part of ongoing strategy. "It's a constant review, not just an opportunistic review," says Tomlinson. He suggests other associations not only look internally but also externally to improve their relevance associated with the area of interest they are trying to serve.

Though not all associations are currently positioned to be able to operate like SME, strategic boards make it easier to do. Strategy that emerges from strength increases the likelihood of success as you provide services to members in an arena where they are already used to seeing and relying on you.

CHAPTER FOUR

Concentrate Resources

> *"It sounds unbelievable, and yet is has happened a hundred times over, that troops have been divided and separated merely according to some vague sense of how things are conventionally done, without a clear understanding of why it is being done.... There is no higher or simpler law for strategy than keeping one's forces concentrated."*
> — CARL VON CLAUSEWITZ[21]

Focus is the act of channeling an organization's energy and activity on a central point. Focus doesn't just happen. It takes analysis and judgment. It takes discipline. And once you have it, losing focus is easy. Over time different ideas, new opportunities, unexpected diversions, or energetic volunteers with a vision can all lure an association away from its focus.

Let's face it. The typical association, regardless of size, profession, or industry, is likely to be all over the lot when it comes to programs, services, products, and activities. Show us an association with a narrow focus, and we will show you an industry anomaly. Focus is a foreign word in association land.

Just check the websites of an association or two. Start with annual meetings, conventions, and trade shows. Then add educational conferences, seminars, workshops, and webinars. Next, view magazines, publications, newsletters, blogs, and various "alerts." Add directories, online networks, and job boards. Mix in public policy advocacy, legislative lobbying, regulatory affairs, and political action. Consider standard setting, industry guidelines, professional ethics, certification, and accreditation. Expand the list to include research, market statistics, operating ratios, and salary surveys. Add marketing, public relations, community outreach, and social responsibility. Include insurance and risk management programs. And finally, toss in group discount programs on everything from car rentals to office supplies to tickets to Disneyland, and you've got a typical menu of association offerings.

Whoops! We failed to mention the member engagement business associations are in: board, houses of delegates, committees, chapters, regions, task forces, special interest groups, sections, councils, and commissions. Now the list is more complete.

The aspirations of associations to undertake so much for their industry or profession could be seen as admirable. Many would laud this well-intentioned quest to do everything possible to help a member in every conceivable area.

In our opinion, it is reckless and thoughtless. In a word: foolhardy.

Perhaps in kinder, gentler times associations could manage a large portfolio of services and activities in a meaningful way. But those days are long gone. Associations are now confronted with the new normal. Its roots probably go back as far as the late 1970s or early 1980s. Since that time, as we mentioned earlier, six high-impact changes have irreversibly changed the landscape for associations—time pressures, value expectations, competition, market changes, generational values, and technology. This is an environment that is far more challenging, far more difficult, and ruthlessly unkind to naïve players.

Set aside five of these trends and focus for a moment on the unprecedented competitive environment associations find themselves in. This new era of competition is, by itself, sufficient to strongly test the "broad-range-of-services" mindset of association executives and volunteer leaders.

More competition means it's difficult to excel in any one area much less in several. Success is unlikely without strategically concentrating resources.

There is an aspect to the competitive environment that is unique to associations. In our work, we have been perplexed by an attitude expressed by many of our association clients: "We really don't have any competition."

Actually, we're a little more than perplexed at this thinking. More like stunned. Granted, few associations have another association that is a direct competitor offering identical services to the same member market. This may be the basis for the "we don't have competition" perspective. But few associations are all alone in their member market, particularly with the recent increase in the number of specialty associations. Take a look at association competition today.

Association Versus Association

The number of associations has grown significantly, many of them targeting a specific segment or niche in an industry or profession. For example, 147 medical specialties now divide medicine into a complex group of physician organizations. As a result, fewer than 19 percent of the physicians in the United States are members of the American Medical Association.

According to Marilen Reimer, CAE, executive director of the American Council of Engineering Companies of Colorado, there are more than 25 technical associations in Colorado and more than 40 others an engineer could belong to. (See the sidebar on page 44 for the complete list.)

Association Members Versus Association. More and more, members of associations offer services that compete with the association. This is particularly true of associate or supplier members, many of whom use free continuing education programs to build relationships with members. Other members use their expertise within the trade or profession to provide coaching or consulting services. Still others offer newsletters, blogs, and/or webinars as a way to build a marketing list for products and services of interest to the membership.

Publishing or Media Companies Versus Association. Publishing and media companies have traditionally competed with associations in the magazine or newsletter space. But as the shift to digital delivery threatens

Potential Association Competitors

Marilen Reimer, CAE, executive director, American Council of Engineering Companies (ACEC) of Colorado, conducted a comprehensive list of competitors in her state. Her analysis consisted of two lists: direct competitors and indirect competitors.

Her direct competitors included the following 25 professional engineering organizations operating Colorado chapters that compete for membership and also provide information, education, advocacy, and networking:

1. American Society of Civil Engineers
2. American Society of Mechanical Engineers
3. Institute of Electrical and Electronics Engineers
4. Colorado Association of Geotechnical Engineers
5. American Society of Heating, Refrigeration, Air Conditioning Engineers
6. Structural Engineers Association of Colorado
7. American Water Works Association
8. Society of Mining, Metallurgy and Exploration
9. Colorado Concrete Specification Institute
10. Illuminating Engineering Society
11. Institute of Transportation Engineers
12. Floodplain Management Association
13. Women in Sustainable Energy
14. Society of Wetland Scientists
15. Society of Fire Protection Engineers
16. American Society of Plumbing Engineers
17. Professional Land Surveyors of Colorado
18. Rocky Mountain Association of Energy Engineers
19. Rocky Mountain Association of Environmental Professionals
20. National Society of Professional Engineers
21. Colorado Association of Black Professional Engineers and Scientists
22. Society of Asian Scientists and Engineers
23. Society of Hispanic Professional Engineers
24. Society of Women Engineers
25. Society of Women Environmental Professionals

ACEC of Colorado's indirect competing associations included more than 40 associations. Some attract engineering companies as associate or supplier members, offering them access to potential clients. Others offer certifications that engineers or companies pursue. All compete for the ACEC of Colorado's members' time and money:

1. Chambers of Commerce
2. Offices of Economic Development
3. American Public Works Association
4. American Institute of Architects
5. Urban Land Institute
6. U.S. Green Building Council
7. Design Build Institute of America
8. Colorado Contractors Association
9. Associated General Contractors of Colorado
10. Hispanic Contractors of Colorado
11. Rocky Mountain Minority Contractors Association
12. Colorado Water Congress
13. Conference of Minority Transportation Officials
14. Move Colorado
15. Home Builders Association
16. Society of Marketing Professional Services
17. Colorado Oil and Gas Association
18. Colorado Municipal League

19. Colorado Counties Inc.
20. National Federation of Independent Businesses
21. American Subcontractors Association
22. Lean Construction Institute
23. American Planners Association
24. Rocky Mountain Electrical League
25. Women in Design
26. Women in Construction
27. American Health Facilities Association
28. Colorado Ground Water Association
29. American Society of Landscape Architecture
30. Water Environment Federation
31. American Water Resources Association
32. Facilities Managers Association
33. Colorado Watershed Assembly
34. Women in Engineering Pro Network
35. Geological Society of America
36. Women in Transportation Seminar
37. Colorado Cleantech Industry Association
38. Engineers Without Borders
39. Habitat for Humanity
40. ACE (Architects/Contractors/Engineers) Mentoring Program

Members are more likely to belong to the one association that provides the most value rather than belonging to two, three, or more associations. And when they do belong to more than one, the associations compete for dues dollars, meeting attendance, sponsors, readership, and volunteer contributions.

◇◇

their core print business, they are expanding into areas like education, job boards, online networks, and insurance. When accessing offerings online, it's sometimes difficult to tell which offerings are from a for-profit company and which are from an association.

Co-ops or Buying Groups Versus Associations. Co-ops start by pooling individual or company buying power to negotiate discounts with suppliers. Membership often results in receiving a rebate check once or twice a year—a powerful value proposition. Next thing you know, they start having meetings, providing education, offering online networks, and disseminating information.

Social Media Versus Associations. As of this writing, Facebook has surpassed 1 billion members and LinkedIn has 175 million members. There are hundreds of smaller niche social networks like Pheed, CyPop, LiveJournal, Tagged, Orkut, Pinterest, ArtStack, SportsYapper, and Instagram. More have undoubtedly emerged since the time we put the finishing touches on this manuscript.

The social media phenomenon has taken a bite out of the networking franchise that the association community once owned. While associations are now making inroads in capitalizing on social media, there is no question that associations missed an incredible opportunity when social networks initially emerged. People now have efficient ways to communicate, interact, and organize without the help of traditional associations.

Internet Versus Associations. The internet has been a game changer for every industry, profession, and association. Here is a competitor that is everywhere, 24 hours a day, providing instant responses mostly for free. Now that's a serious competitor! Consider the impact of search engines alone. They provide robust sources of information in fractions of a second. This provides immediate access to a host of competitive alternatives that members didn't even know existed in the past, making it increasingly difficult for associations to be in the forefront of being "in the know."

In a new twist, online endeavors are now moving into the face-to-face arena. Match.com has launched "Stir" events nationwide. According to promotional material, "When you go to a Stir event, everyone will be single, everyone will be looking to meet someone, and each event will be customized through our group matching algorithms in terms of age, gender, and interests. Stir will be hosting happy hours, cooking classes, wine and tequila tastings, bowling nights, and dance lessons." (Note the use of technology to enhance value.)

So how does this compete with your association? On two levels: First, it's another plea for members' time and second, it is delivering face-to-face events, a method of connection that associations once dominated.

Though your association isn't likely in the matchmaking business, there's something to be learned from Match.com. Notice that the company is creating fun events where it's easy to mix and mingle. Compare this with a typical association meeting where members file in, sit down, and listen. How can you help members more easily meet one another? How can you make things more comfortable for everyone? In short, how can you make your meetings fun? These are questions worth asking, especially as competition continues to increase. We've noticed that associations that have fun have more energy, enthusiasm, and, perhaps most important, higher levels of member participation and engagement.

Time Pressures Versus Associations. The fight for members' time has become one of the most critical battlegrounds for associations. Time pressures come from multiple fronts: dual-career families, work and practice pressures, volunteer commitments, family and friends, recreation and leisure. Don't underestimate the impact of the time famine.

To help you understand your competition, use a competitive analysis matrix. Completing it will provide staff and volunteers with a good synopsis of the competitive landscape, how your association is positioned, and where opportunities might exist.

Competitive Analysis Matrix

Competitor	Competitive Products or Services Offered	Primary Customer	Distribution Method(s)	Strengths	Weaknesses	Strategy	Pricing	Overall Ranking

The competitive analysis matrix above is designed to provide association staff and volunteers with a snapshot of the competitive landscape. First, list all sources of competition for your association's programs, services, products, and activities. In many cases, the list can be exhaustive (but illuminating!) so you may want to first concentrate on the most significant. Next, identify what they offer that competes with you; the customers that they serve, and their primary means of distribution. Then evaluate their strengths, weaknesses, and your perspectives regarding their overall strategy.

Once your competitors and their characteristics are listed, you can then conduct a forced-choice ranking to determine who your most significant competitors are. Under the "Overall Ranking" column, you should assign a number from 1 to 5 to each competitor. A "5" is the highest rating for your strongest competitor and a "1" the lowest. However, you must assign ratings limited by your rating quota. To determine your rating quota, divide the number of competitors by 5.

Let's say you have 10 competitors. Dividing by 5 gives you a rating quota of 2. This means you can give only two competitors the strongest "5" rating, two competitors a "4" rating, and so on. We recommend that you fill in your two "5s" first, then the lowest two "1s." Then go back and fill in two "4s." Next fill in the two "2s," and finally, two "3s." Understanding where your strongest competition is coming from, along with where your products and services are the weakest, will be enlightening. In many cases, the exercise will confirm existing strategy or lead you to a new one.

The Power of Focus

In today's environment of unparalleled competition, an association has to be focused. Competing on multiple fronts is futile. Being spread across numerous product and service lines is a recipe for failure. Being a little bit of this and a little bit of that is not a viable or sustainable option. The typical association has limited, and in many cases, diminishing resources.

To emphasize how important it is not to underestimate the impact of competition, take a look at what Chris Zook found in a 2004 growth survey of 259 executives worldwide: 60 percent reported that their primary source of competitive advantage in their core business was eroding rapidly; 65 percent said that they would need to fundamentally restructure the commercial model they used to serve their core customers; and 72 percent believed that their primary competitor in five years would not be the company that was currently their primary competitor.[22]

Those surveyed were leaders of for-profit companies, presumably adequately financed and staffed. Yet look at the high percentage challenged by the competition! Look at their acknowledgement that their model needed to change. Contrast that with the typical association: often underfunded, possibly understaffed, and likely unfocused.

To perform in today's competitive environment, associations must purposefully concentrate resources on key result areas. This will require a level of discipline heretofore unknown in the association community. It will require that boards understand the unfavorable consequences of dispersing resources across multiple association offerings. It will require the association to answer the concentration question.

In his classic 1973 book, *Management: Tasks, Responsibilities, Practices,* Peter Drucker states, "Wherever we find a business that is outstandingly successful, we will find that it has thought through the concentration alternatives and has made a concentration decision…. The concentration decision is highly risky. It is a genuine decision. It has to be tested again and again against the market, its dynamics, its trends, and its changes."[23]

Associations will have to reverse decades of a something-for-everyone, the-more-the-better, and let's-add-more operating philosophies and make some difficult decisions if they are to perform well in the future. And this will be a considerable challenge. A false safety net is associated with a broad range of diverse services, and making a concentration decision brings risk. It is easy to make an argument for a robust product and service line but difficult to explain why the association is not providing specific services so that it can perform better in the most important ones.

The association community has a large population of small associations. For example, many state and local associations have annual revenues in the $300,000 to $600,000 range, while many national associations operate on budgets of $1 to $2 million. For smaller associations, the concentration decision is even more important. As Drucker says, "Actually, a small company [read: association] needs the concentration decision even more than a big one. Its resources are limited and it will produce no results unless concentrated."[24]

Concentrating resources is especially important in the inception and early growth stages for associations. The Gender Identity Center of Colorado is an example of how powerful concentrating resources can be. Established in 1978, the association was funded by door fees at weekly support group meetings and run by volunteers for the first 33 years of its life. Growth was limited by volunteer capabilities. It wasn't until a decision was made to focus on strengths and harness resources that sustainable expansion occurred. Today it has received grant money, is directed by a part-timer paid $500 per month, and is now staffed with volunteers 10 to 12 hours per day, Monday through Saturday. Interns and pro-bono counselors provide private counseling, and the organization is using Skype and instant messaging to broaden its reach. Using technology and never wavering from its founding purpose of providing support to transgendered people (its core strength) has enabled the organization to stabilize and grow.

Even a niche organization like the Gender Identity Center has competition. It competes for funding and volunteer time with broader based lesbian, gay, bisexual, and transgender groups. Do not define your competition too narrowly. The concentration decision must take into account an accurate and complete assessment of all competitive factors confronting your association.

Fighting Competition with Concentration

In order to concentrate resources, today's association needs a process that results in leadership consensus about the areas most important to the association's future. In essence, it needs to answer the following questions:

- What, if done, will make a significant difference for the member? How can the association address a significant member issue or problem, meet a need, or otherwise add member value?

- What would significantly strengthen the association's capability to serve members?

- Where should the association focus its resources for the maximum return to the member?

Believe it or not, there exists such a process. It's called strategic planning. We like Drucker's definition of strategic planning: "the application of thought, analysis, imagination, and judgment."[25] In short, it provides the answer to how to make the concentration decision.

We'll admit that no management tool has been subjected to more question, opinion, derision, and ridicule. When we Googled "strategic planning is dead" in December 2012, there were 4,280,000 results! At the same time, others credit strategic planning with being critical to their success.

The criticism and dismissal of strategic planning is puzzling. We have never heard anyone dismiss meeting planning as a waste of time. No one disparages financial planning. Retirement planning is seen as an important tool. Even wedding planning and vacation planning are seen positively! And we have to ask the critics and the nonbelievers: If strategic planning is not an effective management activity, why is it one of the seven criteria for performance excellence for the Malcolm Baldrige National Quality Award? We've seen—time and time again—how the process builds consensus, creates energy, and focuses association teams.

Those who have struggled with the process rejoiced in 1994 when Henry Mintzberg rigorously challenged the 1960s model of strategic planning in "The Fall and Rise of Strategic Planning," published in *Harvard Business Review*.[26] Mintzberg was the first to challenge the model of strategic planning used by many large corporations in the mid-1960s. It is important to go beyond the headlines and understand what he was critical of and the changes he proposed.

Mintzberg challenged the ability of large departments staffed with strategic planners that developed plans for execution by management. He referred to this as "strategic programming" and noted that the plans developed neither directed management activity nor produced the expected results.

We see this play out in associations when strategic planning committees—rather than the board—spend time and energy preparing a plan that they won't execute and that, though approved by the board, doesn't truly become adopted by the board in a way that informs its decisions or influences resource allocation. People support what they help create, and boards that don't do the work of strategic planning often don't have adequate buy-in. It's easy for the plan to become just another document to approve rather than one to live by when the board isn't intimately involved in its creation.

Mintzberg believed that this structured process, removed from the realities of markets, customers, and competitors, should be replaced by what he called "strategic thinking." He defined this as "capturing what the manager learns from all sources (both the soft insight from his or her personal experiences and the experiences of others throughout the organization and the hard data from market research and the line) and then synthesizing that learning into a vision of the direction that the business should pursue."[27]

It's not enough for volunteer leaders to create and approve a plan. Associations that are thriving make sure their senior staff is fully involved in the process, buy into the plan, and are committed to implementation. We've scratched our heads more than once when working with a board that either didn't want senior staff in a planning retreat or that wanted them there but didn't want them to participate.

Huh? These are some of the association's most valuable human assets. They live the association day in and day out. They interact with members daily on the phone, respond to member queries, represent the association in meetings, handle media queries, and most likely know more about the association than any volunteer possibly can. We believe not involving them in the planning process is a grave mistake.

Mintzberg contends that strategic thinking is about synthesis. And we agree. It is a combination of analysis, forecasting, testing, and reacting. And while off-site retreats can be a critical step in the process, strategic planning requires much more than a retreat. There's this thing called implementation where we see many associations fall short.

Glenn Tecker weighed in on the strategic plan debate in "The Future of Planning for the Future," in the April 2012 issue of *Associations Now* as follows:

> I think what is necessary is clarity and consensus around a number of decisions. One of the decisions is, "What is the purpose for this organization existing?" The second is, "What are we trying to accomplish

as an organization?" The third is, "What path will we take to accomplish those things?" and then the fourth is, "How will we know if it's working?" To me, it's less important what you call the answers to those questions than that you have a continuous conversation about what the answers will be.[28]

So whether it is called "strategic planning" or "strategic thinking," the process is critical to the concentration decision. And if there is one criticism of strategic planning that most would agree with, it is that a plan that gathers dust is as bad as no plan at all.

Another criticism of the planning process is that it can be viewed simply as an event where everyone comes together; etches objectives, strategies, and action plans in stone; and marches off in a tightly scripted, carefully prescribed direction, despite a changing environment. This is folly. Things happen. People learn from experience. Successes open new doors. Failures are instructive. Sometimes you even get a lucky break— one that was never even considered during the planning process.

In *The Effective Executive*, Peter Drucker wrote, "Napoleon allegedly said that no successful battle ever followed its plan. Yet Napoleon also planned every one of his battles, far more meticulously than any earlier general had done."[29] Napoleon knew that the perfect plan didn't exist. Yet he continued to do his best to craft one, knowing full well that it would require adjustments, reactions, and changes as events on the battlefield unfolded.

Is Focus Un-Association-Like?

We recently followed a blog discussing the topic of "what associations do better than anyone else." The discussion was initiated by ASAE senior editor Joe Rominiecki with the following question: "If your association had to decide which one product or service it was best at providing and from then on produce that one item alone and nothing else, what would it be?"

Of course, this dialogue was music to our ears.

> "I worry that this lack of focus in associations might prevent them from achieving a Dyson-level of quality—the level of 'we're the best in the world and we guarantee it'—in any particular product or service. Of course, any given association could, theoretically, pick

one of its offerings, eschew the rest, and pursue it at the highest level. And the particular offering chosen would likely be different at every association, depending on each one's unique circumstances and skill sets."[30]

One post challenged a single-service approach for associations. It asked if an association would discontinue being an association if it decided to focus on just one service or product, suggesting that the essence of an association is the provision of a variety of services, products, and activities for a community of members.

The "package of services" idea is what gets many associations in trouble, unless it is very deliberately constructed. Concentrating on fewer, more meaningful services will improve the association's competitive position, streamline and strengthen its communications, and simplify the infrastructure required to maintain, sell, and deliver its key benefits. It frees resources to be used on strengthening strengths. The concept of focused services creates a stronger future for the average association.

Contrary to the thinking that the essence of an association is a range of products and services, many effective associations are focused on a few key deliverables. For instance, the National Association of Manufacturers is in one business and one business alone: advocacy. The Air Movement and Control Association (AMCA) has a mission to "advance the health, growth, and integrity" of its industry. AMCA has narrowed its strategic objective list to three under this umbrella (certifying product ratings, regionalizing support operations to better serve Asian and European members, and lobbying code authorities). Everything else AMCA does supports its mission and these three broad strategic objectives. And the Metal Treating Institute focuses on only five: benchmarking and forecasting, training for industry compliance, meetings, 24/7 connection, and a resource library. Anything else falls outside its area of strength.

Are you envious? Thinking, "There's no way my association could do this." Or are you energized by the concept and wondering how your association could concentrate resources? Read on to learn how.

Case Study

The Power of Focus

ASSOCIATION: National Association of Manufacturers (NAM)

BUDGET: $35 Million

NUMBER OF STAFF MEMBERS: 135

NUMBER OF MEMBERS: 12,000

The National Association of Manufacturers is an anomaly. In a landscape of associations that offer a wide variety of products and services, it focuses on one: advocacy. The focus allows this broad-based association to find common ground among members as diverse as chemical companies, automobile makers, and airplane manufacturers.

Rather than addressing industry-specific issues, NAM focuses on broader business topics as a means of finding common areas of interest among members. Rick Klein, senior vice president, chief financial officer and treasurer, notes, "We focus on issues across industry lines, such as tax and trade issues. We don't get into the specifics of any particular industry. We're looking at the bigger, higher level issues that affect all of manufacturing."

Like other associations, at one time NAM attempted to increase member value by offering a variety of programs and services, including insurance. Says Klein, "We found we were pushing services rather than having people want us to provide them, and we weren't being all that successful. For example, we had a couple of insurance programs but because insurance is really written on an industry-specific basis with almost industry-specific carriers, we didn't have the demand." Further, the association's offerings were similar to other association offerings. Klein notes, "We had a couple of programs that were just the same as anybody else's. We concluded it's not worth our time to support them in any great way because the demand isn't there." Based on this experience, NAM no longer offers insurance.

Concentrating resources takes discipline. "If you're not disciplined with your plan and your budget, you can really be all over the place pretty quickly," advises Klein. The association surveys members annually, uses a strategic plan, and depends on the budgeting process to reflect priorities. Taken together, these three basic tenets further the interests and effectiveness of the organization, but not without tests. Says Klein, "We ask, 'How is this going to support our objectives, and is it going to support enough of our membership that it means we should move forward with it?'"

The tight focus requires input from member companies about the effect of moving forward on any issue and what it would mean to the membership overall. NAM's policy statements serve as a compass for advocacy efforts by both NAM members and staff. Klein notes, "You can get factions on boards that will tie you in knots and send you in different directions." Preventing that requires a great deal of trust and a strong partnership between the board and staff. Observes Jay Timmons, president and CEO, "At NAM, policy making begins and ends with our members. Our policy-making structure and process ensures that the views expressed by the association represent a broad cross-section of the leaders of the manufacturing economy."

Staff obviously plays a large part when it comes to remaining focused on goals and objectives. To this end, NAM has a staff incentive compensation plan. Payment is based on two things: individual goals and overall effectiveness of the organization. The plan is another way the NAM concentrates resources on what it deems most important to its members.

Similar to other associations, NAM wrestles with the issues of degree. Not many initiatives are suggested that won't help the organization in some way, but the question is, "To what degree?" The challenge is to determine which will support the association's goals in a big way versus which will support it in a small way and to concentrate resources on the former. For NAM, advocacy is the clear winner.

CHAPTER FIVE

The Concentration Decision

*"My success, part of it certainly, is that I
have focused in on a few things."*
— BILL GATES[31]

To compete successfully in the new normal, association executives and volunteer leaders are going to have to break a long-standing habit of saying yes to virtually everything. Staff feels compelled to agree with new ideas or new initiatives proposed by boards or committees regardless of the dispersion of resources that will result. If they balk, they risk being accused of being negative or not being innovative or just trying to avoid work. Volunteers are reluctant to challenge a peer's proposal. It's just easier to say yes. It is politically correct. It reflects a positive attitude. It demonstrates openness to ideas. But "yes" is simply not the right answer in many cases.

Association executives and volunteers need permission to say no. They must understand the consequences of accepting every new idea, every new initiative, every request for assistance, every proposal for a partnership, every additional member benefit. Associations must understand the value of saying no and the critical impact it has on the imperative of concentrating resources and focusing attention on what is most important.

Maybe a slight variation of "just say no" is in order. Perhaps we have to recognize that many well-intentioned proposals are legitimate. They would add value. They would have a sound purpose. They would serve a worthy cause. So perhaps we should say, "Yes, that is a good idea, but if we continue to pursue every good idea that comes along, we will be spread so thin that we will marginalize everything we do." Or, "Yes, that is a good idea, but every hour that staff is working on that project is an hour that staff is not working on our number-one priority." Or, "Yes, that is a good idea, but every dollar spent on it is a dollar we don't spend on the areas that we agree we should concentrate on."

What Even Simple New Programs Involve

One reason association offerings increase is that the time, effort, and energy to support a new idea is often underestimated. A new program is suggested and supported with the contention, "Why not? It won't take that much."

Let's assume a discount program has been recommended. A provider has agreed to offer a discount to members and a rebate to the association for the volume of business generated. A slam dunk. It's a good deal for the member and the association gets nondues revenue. And best of all, "It won't take that much." Here is a quick summary of the eight things that have to take place to make such a new program happen:

1. The association has to do due diligence on the provider, vetting the quality of the product or service and verifying the legitimacy of the discount compared to competitive offerings. It probably should check other providers to see if they can get an even better deal.

2. The association has to negotiate the arrangements: How much is the rebate? When is it paid? How do we track member purchases?

3. The association has to develop the process by which transactions will be handled. Will the member place the order to the association or directly to the vendor? How will the mechanics of the transaction be handled?

4. The association has to determine how member complaints will be handled if there is any dissatisfaction.

5. The association has to write and proof promotional copy and place advertisements in the newsletter, magazine, website, and/or at the association's meetings.

6. The association has to monitor sales.

7. The association has to verify sales and collect the rebates.

8. Over time, the association will have to update promotion as the provider makes changes to the product or service.

The above eight steps show how complicated and time-intensive "It won't take much" can really be.

Using a Strategic Plan to Guide Concentration Decisions

In an effort to concentrate resources, many associations use their strategic plans to vet new ideas or recommendations. Plans can be misused, however. We have been amazed and amused at how imaginative volunteers and staff can be at linking their new initiative to one of the goals or objectives in the plan. "Our proposed community outreach isn't a priority in the plan, but it does involve a social media component that aligns with the priority to capitalize on internet technologies."

Though we see strategic plans as documents that discipline staff and leaders to focus on what's most important, some express concerns that a strategic plan is a straightjacket that inhibits creativity and innovation. We believe John Kao addressed this well when he said:

> You have to do some degree of strategic planning by definition, because you have to decide what you're going to do, what resources you're going to apply, what your expectations are around success, who's going to be responsible, and what the metrics are for returns. But if the strategic plan becomes a prison so that you can't respond to something because you say, "Oh, well, the strategic plan doesn't allow that," then you're in big trouble. Strategic planning, if practiced intelligently, is an essential part of what an organization needs to do. The trick from an innovation perspective is to make sure that the innovation agenda is appropriately represented in the strategic planning process.[32]

Deliberate and Intentional Consideration

In addition to having permission to say no, we also believe that associations benefit when there's a process in place for deliberate and intentional consideration of new products and services. Consider the Florida Bar's Program and Evaluation Committee's description:

> This committee provides the Board of Governors with: (1) guide-lines and standards by which Florida Bar programs are reviewed or evaluated, (2) in-depth evaluations of selected Bar programs, (3) recommendations relating to proposed new or expanded programs, (4) review of programs for resource and budgetary appropriations, (5) The Florida Bar's program descriptions, and (6) coordination with the Strategic Planning Committee and the Budget Committee.
>
> The Director of Planning and Evaluation prepares in-depth evaluation reports on those programs selected by the committee for detailed study. The committee reviews the reports and recommendations and submits its report to the Board. Program descriptions for all Bar programs are developed by the Director of Planning and Evaluation and reviewed by the committee to determine the agenda for programs to be evaluated. The Program Evaluation Committee works closely with the Budget Committee in reviewing and evaluating programs. Proponents of new programs are required to submit a detailed program proposal and a budget for review by the Program Evaluation Committee. A detailed three-year budget projection must then be submitted to the Budget Committee.

Notice the requirement for a detailed program proposal, the coordination between committees, and the three-year budget projection. Deliberate? Yes? Intentional? Yes. Wise? Very. Developing a deliberate process helps concentrate resources.

The Imperative for Technology Concentration

There is one area of resource concentration that few, if any, can avoid: technology. As we mentioned in the previous chapter, technology is a strength for few associations. The common association "technologies" are person-to-person meetings, ink-on-paper communication, and maybe a member-specific database. The relevant association of tomorrow must master digital technologies and the internet. Every association must concentrate resources on this essential effort.

A first step is to analyze your association's technology spend, the percentage of your total annual revenue, both payroll and nonpayroll, that is spent on technology. Add up what you spend (salaries, benefits, and overhead) on IT staff, whether in house or with independent contractors. Then add to this what you spend on webhosting, computers, servers, database, and any other associated costs. This is your technology spend. Based on our research, the average association spends 4.1 percent of its annual revenue on all aspects of technology. A review of other industries published by CXO Media indicates that tech spends range from 1.7 percent to 8.6 percent. Take a look:

IT Spending by Industry

Financial Services	8.6%
Government, Education and Nonprofit	5.5%
Healthcare	4.4%
Manufacturing and Transportation	2.6%
Retail	1.7%

(Copyright 2011. CXO Media Inc. Reprinted with permission. All rights reserved.)[33]

Further, in the 10th annual survey of *CIO* magazine, published in January 2011, 17 percent of 729 top IT executives at their company or business units indicated that IT spend is 8 percent or more of total company revenue.

Without getting bogged down in the numbers, it is clear that the successful association of the future will have to concentrate considerably more resources on technology, probably in the range of 10 percent of total revenues, if not more. One group we worked with recently agreed to put 17 percent of its total annual revenue toward technology!

Increasing technology spending is not going to be easy. First, you have to convince directors, many of whom are not early adopters, to increase the percentage spent on technology. Often, you're asking them to commit financial resources to things they don't fully understand. Second, technologies are changing and evolving at an accelerating rate and associations are typically slow, deliberate, and averse to risk. Wresting resources away from other programs and activities is challenging, as all have constituencies (member, volunteer, and staff) likely to resist. Finally, the average association doesn't have the expertise necessary to comfortably make technology a priority. Getting the expertise may mean outsourcing.

The Role of the CEO

The one person who most needs permission to say no is the association CEO. If anybody needs to have the discipline to make the difficult decisions to maintain a concentration of resources on the most important things, it is the CEO. That's because most board chairs or chief elected officers did not pursue their leadership positions to tell peers and members that the association is not going to accept their ideas or implement their proposals. The officers or board may hold the line for a while, but it's difficult not to cave in to pressure to approve proposals or recommendations.

The political environment is unkind to people with the discipline to say no. Quite the contrary, the association political environment loves the yes-man or the yes-woman. They have a lot of friends and their political base can be considerable. Everybody gets what they want. Everybody's happy. As a result, the association's programs sprawl. Its services expand. Its resources are dispersed. Its competitive position erodes. Its value is diminished. And too often the volunteer leader goes off the board, waves goodbye, and leaves the association to figure it out—and it all begins again with the election of a new leader or board.

Let's be realistic. Through no fault of their own, board members make decisions for which they will not be held accountable. They don't have an annual review. They are not compensated based on their performance. And many spend only one term on the board before moving on to the next volunteer assignment, often with another organization. As one exec said, "We have directors that will go off the board in a month or two making decisions that staff will have to live with for years, some for careers."

How many board members have voted approval of the introduction or pursuit of a major new program or service in their last meeting as a director? And as they made their decision, how many of them were thoughtfully considering the resource implications? The alignment with the association's strategic direction? The consequences on the association's concentration decision?

Of course, many volunteers take their work seriously and hold themselves accountable. There just aren't enough of them. And all it takes is one board member to put a half-baked idea on the table and away we go introducing something new, sometimes without adequate financial support or marketing plans. Instead, we too often rely on the "Field of Dreams" method: If we build it, they will come.

The volunteer dynamic (working with peers and "here today, gone tomorrow") requires the CEO to be the steward of resource concentration. CEOs need to use—and the board has to empower them to use—the following techniques to focus the association's resources on key result areas to hold the association true to its concentration decision:

Ask the important questions. Questions should test the new idea, request, recommendation, or proposal against the concentration decision. Is this initiative really worth drawing resources from our agreed-upon priorities? Is this really worth diverting scarce resources from the key result areas that we have agreed to pursue? Have we adequately analyzed what resources this will require?

Compile data. Too many board decisions lack sound data. The CEO must demonstrate the resource consequences of ideas, requests, recommendations, or proposals with facts about the dollars and cents—the human resources (both volunteer and staff), the marketing and communication costs, and the expected break-even point (assuming there is one).

Picture the alternative. Show graphically how the sum of the resources for the idea would look if allocated to the association's concentration priority. "OK, you are willing to spend ___ dollars and allocate ___ hours of volunteer and staff time and commit ___ dollars in marketing and promotion. If we allocated this to what we currently agree is our most important initiative, our area of agreed concentration, this is what we could accomplish in the first year: _____."

For real success, the CEO needs a board that is a partner in the concentration strategy. Unfortunately, most boards are composed for everything but this kind of performance. Boards composed geographically, by special interest, by who you know or how long you've been hanging around are unlikely to come together to support a focused approach in directing the association. This is why we are advocates of small, competency-based boards and boards with directors selected for specific skills, knowledge, or other qualifications, including discipline, the ability to govern (not micromanage) conscientiously and apply rigor in directing the association's activities and resources, and the willingness to say no when necessary. What CEO would not want directors like this on their team?

Most boards fumble the concentration decision. Their large size makes them vulnerable to political influences and personal persuasion. Their built-in discontinuity makes it extremely difficult to sustain a concentration strategy. They rarely appreciate the power of focus. Focus isn't fun—until you begin to reap the significant rewards it can produce. Most boards will not have the discipline and patience to let the concentration decision play out and perform unless they empower the CEO to hold their feet to the fire.

Role of the Board

Enlightened board members partner with the CEO to make wise concentration decisions, recognizing that limited resources (the reality for most associations) demand difficult and deliberate decisions. They are willing to take the time to identify strengths and focus on activities that promise the highest return on investment, both for members and the association as a whole.

A board can help with the concentration decision by:

Asking questions. Like the CEO, board members should get in the habit of questioning options and decisions. Questions help ensure opportunities aren't missed and are a safe way to work through decisions that can be potentially divisive. Unity and clarity of purpose are necessary for healthy board functioning. Asking—and carefully answering—questions creates consensus and comfort as board members (sometimes representing different constituencies) listen to and learn from one another. Often, the deeper the questioning, the more certain the resulting decision.

Relying on staff. Listen to the association's paid professionals, but don't be afraid to question them to verify that data and assumptions are solid. Recognize good work when you see it. Hold staff accountable for presenting thoroughly crafted proposals and fully vetted recommendations. Let them be responsible for due diligence but don't abdicate your responsibility to make sure all the bases are covered.

Deciding to decide. It's easy to postpone decisions when there's lack of consensus or there's strong disagreement among board members. But refusing to make a concentration decision potentially weakens the association's position and value proposition. It also may mean offering under-resourced and/or mediocre member benefits.

Being willing to let go. Are there products and services that are past their prime or never lived up to expectations to begin with? Are others stale and need updating? Perhaps some were ill-conceived from the outset but were approved as a courtesy. Allowing programs to limp along is a drag on resources, uses valuable staff time, and clutters communication to members. We've heard many CEOs and board presidents say, "We should have done that a long time ago," after they see new energy, enthusiasm, and possibility when activities are discontinued to concentrate resources elsewhere.

Strategies for Success

Because concentrating resources is still new for many associations, it will likely take time and practice to turn this focus into a habit. Don't underestimate the difficulty in creating a new routine. The gravitational pull of "business as usual" and "the way we've always done it," will be strong. Staff and volunteers alike will have to be reminded that "business as unusual" is the new normal and that "the way we've always done it" doesn't work in a more competitive environment. The quickest way to develop a new habit is to show an early success in the resource concentration game. The following tips will help:

1. Don't define the competition too narrowly. A comprehensive, thorough competitive analysis is critically important. Unless the leadership and staff understand the scale and intensity of the competition, they won't have the motivation to seriously and religiously concentrate resources. As part of your strategic planning activity, undertake a rigorous competitive assessment. (The matrix earlier in this chapter will be helpful for doing this.) Challenge leadership and staff to expand the definition of competition and draw wider and wider circles of competitive influence.

Be specific regarding what the competition is doing and how it is affecting you.

2. Don't entertain new programs or activities one at a time. A common practice of associations that gets them spread thin over too many services is considering proposals for new programs at any time. A board member, staff, or committee chair can always put a new idea on the board meeting agenda. So in March they approve an outreach activity. In June they approve a group discount program. Then in September they add an educational seminar to the agenda. And in December they approve a partnership with a related association.

To avoid this program creep, limit the proposal of new ideas or services to one or two selected board meetings a year, ideally the meeting prior to the board meeting where the next year's budget is approved. New programs or products require resources, and they will draw resources away from priorities. If they are all considered at one time, they will have to compete with each other. A board is less likely to vote in a slew of programs and be more cognizant of the total resource commitment required. Don't let well-intentioned volunteers or staff nickel and dime you into resource dispersion. By the same token, don't let this approach be a straightjacket if an opportunity presents itself. A quick analysis should be sufficient to know if an exception is warranted. We think exceptions will be few.

3. Concentrate innovation activity. As we noted previously, innovation is far more than creativity. It is a long road from an idea to a marketable product or service. While there will be times when it is important to brainstorm freely and unfettered, at some point the association will have to apply the concentration decision to its innovative alternatives. An idea needs attention, energy, and funding to become a marketable innovation. If you get spread too thin in your portfolio of potential innovations, you may not get any to actualization.

4. Take a staff head count. Then ask, "What if we focused on only one area? What if all the staff were concentrated on one thing? What might we be able to accomplish if we 'bet the farm' on XYZ?" The answer is likely to be: "A lot more than we are accomplishing today." And that would make an enormous difference. Or consider a department that you believe has significant potential and ask, "What if we increased the membership staff from half a person to three? What would our return be on increased recruitment and improved retention?" Or, "What if we had a full-time director of development with a support staff instead of using a volunteer committee for fundraising? What would our returns be for the foundation?" If the results appear to be significant, the next question has to be, "How can we shift staff positions from other areas to concentrate them on this opportunity?"

Make sure the above questions are designed to focus on strengths or help you concentrate resources. Otherwise, the opportunities you identify may become diversions rather than a means of employing carefully considered strategies designed to strengthen your future as an association.

A final word about concentrating resources: Don't underestimate the power that will be unleashed. Contrast the following with von Clausewitz's observation on generals dispersing their troops at the beginning of this chapter. Eisenhower did not attack the entire coast of France. He concentrated his attack on a 50-mile stretch of Normandy beaches:

> On June 6, 1944, the D-Day operation in Normandy brought together the land, air, and sea forces of the allied armies in what became known as the largest invasion force in human history. The operation, given the code name "Overlord," delivered five naval assault divisions to the beaches of Normandy, France.... The invasion force included 7,000 ships and landing craft manned by over 195,000 naval personnel from eight allied countries. Almost 133,000 troops from England, Canada, and the United States landed on D-Day.... By June 30th, over 850,000 men, 148,000 vehicles, and 570,000 tons of supplies had landed on the Normandy shores.[34]

Concentration is powerful!

CHAPTER SIX

Fit: Integrating Programs and Services

"Fit is a far more central component of competitive advantage than most realize."
– MICHAEL PORTER[35]

Associations offer programs, services, products, and activities. Some of these menus are quite extensive, though a few are narrowly focused. Regardless of the range of offerings, seldom is an association portfolio the result of a master plan for developing or directing the association's program and services. The typical association's benefits package just happens over time. Unfortunately, the result is often a hodgepodge of undifferentiated benefits—a program here, a product there. Few associations have a cohesive, well-thought-out mix of programs and services that are purposefully integrated and that complement and reinforce each other. In short, scarce is the association with a menu of services that takes advantage of synergy.

This shortcoming is understandable because for decades associations have operated in an environment of little competition. For many years there were multiple opportunities to expand the association's product and service line, both internally and externally. It was relatively easy to come up with a program or service, introduce it to your membership, and successfully attract a meaningful number of users or participants.

From the outside, suppliers to the member market saw associations as a means to reach a market. In many instances, the association's endorsement (or implied endorsement) of a vendor's product or service gave it instant credibility. And these suppliers were more than willing to pay a fee, royalty, or commission for the business generated through the association. All the association had to do was include the product or service in its list of benefits, do a little advertising, and collect the commission. Easy money. And the members won as well, getting a better price through the association than on the open market. For the association, this sort of relationship is a no-brainer—or at least it was.

Another external source of expanded offerings came from related associations. They often saw the potential of pooling the memberships of two or three associations to support a joint venture, such as a cosponsored educational conference, a collective public relations initiative, or a partnership on an insurance program. The associations could share the costs, risks, and net revenue. It would certainly be easier than going it alone. And again, members won, getting a benefit that they might not if the association hadn't joined forces with another organization to make it feasible. These opportunities also looked like a cakewalk—at the time.

Competitors are often an instigating factor for a new benefit or offering. A board member or staff will observe that another association is successfully delivering a product or service and think, "Why not us?" It is obviously viable, as the other association's offering is successful and profitable (or so it seems on the surface). It will be a benefit to members and improve recruitment and retention. After all, adding programs, services, products, or activities is part of the association tradition. The increasingly diverse membership has differing needs, so we need more offerings to cover the splintering member market. We have rarely encountered a board that didn't like a new program or service, clinging to the mistaken belief that more "stuff" adds value.

And then there is the ubiquitous siren song of nondues revenue. We have heard, "We need to develop new sources of nondues revenue," in planning sessions countless times. It's hard to argue against more revenue.

But rarely is the pursuit of nondues revenue thought of in the context of what other businesses the association is currently in. (When we say "businesses," we are talking about all the distinct activities and services the association offers.) Whether the nondues opportunity is a good fit is usually irrelevant. It is not even discussed or considered. The sole objective is revenue generation, with little regard for the source, how it fits with other offerings, or how it might further clutter an already unwieldy assortment of programs. Often absent in the discussion is the term "net," as in net revenue. The evaluation of the costs to develop, market, staff, and support the new nondues offering is scant. Only years later is it discovered that the whole venture has been a fool's errand without the desired net results.

What Is Fit?

In an entry in the *Harvard Business Review* blog network, Joan Magretta, a senior associate at the Institute for Strategy and Competitiveness, wrote about Michael Porter's five tests of good strategy. In regard to fit, she said, "Great strategies are like complex systems in which all of the parts fit together seamlessly. Each thing you've chosen to do amplifies the value of the other things you do. That's how fit improves the bottom line. It also enhances sustainability."[36]

To better understand fit, take a look at publishing. What do you think of when you hear the name John Grisham? Legal thrillers. And J.K. Rowling? Young adult fantasy.

Publishers understand the value of fit—especially when they have a bestseller on their hands. Grisham's second book was also a legal thriller; Rowling's was another young adult fantasy. (But not just any young adult fantasy. Another Harry Potter fantasy.) The second books fit with the first and fans weren't confused or disappointed. The bottom line improved; author sustainability was guaranteed. That's the value of fit. If either author had written their second book in a different genre, say Grisham in romance or Rowling in nonfiction, the result may not have been the same and we doubt that Grisham and Rowling would be household names today. As of 2008, Grisham had sold more than 250 million copies worldwide.[37] He's one of only three authors to sell 2 million copies on a first printing. The other two are J.K. Rowling (as of June 2011, she'd sold 450 million copies[38]) and Tom Clancy.[39]

It wasn't until his twelfth book (*A Painted House*), after he had a huge following, that Grisham published anything other than a legal thriller. And J.K. Rowling finished the seven books in the Harry Potter series before changing genres and releasing *The Casual Vacancy,* her foray into adult literature in 2012, seven years after the last in her young adult series.

Line extensions and related service offerings are naturally easier because of established awareness and aligned interest levels. With this in mind, let's take a look at associations.

We once worked with a trade association whose board members bragged about the revenue generated by its major conference and exposition. True, it was a major income generator. But when the Finance Committee and CFO took a closer look, a sobering picture emerged. Although the conference and exposition did generate a surplus after direct costs were charged, staff time and overhead had not been part of the calculation. When conservative estimates of staff and overhead costs were allocated, the true picture emerged. The conference and exposition had been losing money for years. The net was missing from the revenue.

The same was true for a charitable organization we worked with that wisely set a policy that allowed the organization to participate only in fundraisers expected to net a set hourly amount per volunteer hour. Unfortunately, the policy emerged only after a review showed that some events were making less than minimum wage per volunteer hour, despite the fact that many of the organization's volunteers were highly compensated individuals such as Realtors®, physicians, attorneys, and a hospital president! This endeavor clearly was not the best use of volunteers' time and expertise, and the desired results were not achieved. The review of fundraising activities—including staff and overheard—painted a clearer picture and although fundraising was important, it clearly wasn't a good fit with the overall mission of the organization.

A biology society we know of, in search of nondues revenue, designed a lovely calendar featuring photos submitted by members. Optimistic, the group ordered 1,000 and planned to sell them for $15 each, for a gross income of $15,000. As often happens with volunteer-driven groups, they learned (too late) that only student organizations registered with the university could set up a sales table on campus, thus eliminating one of their planned sales routes. As you can imagine, the results were less than stellar. Five highly educated scientists managed to move 350 calendars, producing net revenue of $300 after printing costs. Looking back, the president deemed it a "terribly inefficient use of time." Definitely not a fit with the other program and services offerings and this project didn't even provide value for members.

Contrast the above scenario with Southwest Airlines, a company that made its mark on the airline industry by having a clear vision regarding what fit best into its operating strategy. Writes Walter Kiechel III in *Lords of Strategy,* "In pursuit of its fly-cheap strategy, it had confronted the trade-offs, made the choices, and achieved the fit: only short flights, no meal service or link-ups with other airlines, only one type of aircraft for shorter turnarounds and more time in the air."[40]

Boards aren't the only groups born to recommend ill-considered benefits or initiatives. Committees do the same. Chairs drive their committees to conjure up new ideas with the hope of developing new member benefits or nondues revenue. Their recommendations are rarely rejected. Board members are reluctant to turn down proposals from peers. More services look better than fewer. And there's the "it won't take much" trap. But does the new idea fit? It may not. It may add another unrelated offering to the already cluttered menu.

Staff is in the game as well, from the CEO to department heads to committee liaisons. With today's premium on creating a compelling value proposition, association staffs are aggressively seeking new ways to add value, and the course most often taken is a new service or benefit. Admittedly, some of this effort results in product or service extensions that do fit. But "thinking outside the box" can have the unintended consequence of developing something new that doesn't complement the association's existing product line.

Whether driven by external forces or internal initiatives, the resulting array of most association offerings generally don't fit well together. In fact, in many instances, the only thing that the association's programs and benefits have in common is that they seemed to be a good idea at some point in time.

In his well-known article, "What is Strategy?" Michael Porter writes:

> Strategic fit among many activities is fundamental not only to competitive advantage but also to the sustainability of that advantage. It is harder for a rival to match an array of interlocked activities than it is merely to imitate a particular sales-force approach, match a process technology, or replicate a set of product features. Positions built on systems of activities are far more sustainable than those built on individual activities.[41]

Let's face it. Developing integrated programs and services is much more difficult than tossing out a program here and a service there. It means that associations have to do two things:

Make an honest assessment. Do we offer "interlocked activities" or "systems of activity," or is our service portfolio based on a diverse array of individual activities?

Define and commit to a unifying concept as the basis for a fit strategy. What's your dominant theme or core strength that is the basis for fit? What is your association essentially about? It may be helpful to use Chris Zook's definition of a core business described in Chapter 3 of this book (the association's set of products, capabilities, customers, channels, and geographies).

For example, a trade association could build around the dominant theme of government. This would include lobbying, legislative updates, grassroots activity, campaign support, and PACs. In addition, it would address regulatory advocacy, updates on new regulation, educational offerings focused on compliance strategies, and compliance assistance.

Another trade association concept that could be the basis for fit is market assistance. Typically, an exposition or trade show would be the underpinning of this theme, being a major source of efficiently putting buyers together with sellers. Complementary services and products might include a magazine or newsletter (hopefully digital!) focused on articles about new product/market developments and advertising opportunities, market data, market research and trend studies, publicity programs to drive demand, and global trade missions to explore new markets.

For the professional society, a logical theme is competence in the form of continuing educational programs, professional symposiums, scholarly journals, online networks for professional knowledge transfer, scholarship programs, awards for excellence, and student chapters.

Another theme for individual membership associations is career building, including professional development programs, career ladders and counseling, job boards, document bank (resumé templates, sample contracts, etc.), compensation studies, and mentoring programs.

Complementary services produce fit and, not coincidentally, allow an association to focus on strengths (because they all are in the same arena) and concentrate resources. The five strategies on the road to relevance are designed to create synergy. They fit.

The Healthcare Businesswomen's Association (HBA) found its fit through leadership development for women in the healthcare field. Since its founding in 1979, HBA has offered educational and networking opportunities, recognized outstanding women in the healthcare industry, and served as a conduit for research on career advancement. While HBA was able to deliver high value to those who lived near an operating chapter or could travel to one of its events, it couldn't establish chapters fast enough to serve others who could benefit from its leadership development programs. As a result, the association wanted a platform that would allow for expansion of its membership without the limitations of physical location. In addition, members who attended live events were interested in having a way to continue the conversations and learning that had begun, allowing them to dig deeper into career-enhancing topics over a longer period of time.

HBA developed Leadership Online, a virtual environment that gives the association a unique platform on which it can host online educational sessions, live chat, confidential coaching sessions, teleconferences, "rooms" in which to store reference materials, and other offerings—extending the reach of its unifying concept of leadership for women in healthcare.

"We approached it differently than most organizations that create a virtual environment," says Laurie Cooke, CEO of HBA. "Rather than thinking in terms of a one-day event, we wanted to build a community and encourage engagement over time. We were really looking for something that would feel like our local and global meetings to those who couldn't attend them and give them access to peers and leaders they might otherwise never have the chance to meet. We have only scratched the surface of what Leadership Online can do." Cooke adds, "When we started, we had a target of adding 10 new members as a result of the program. Instead we added 26. Of the roughly 300 participants, 75 percent were senior level or above, with 16 to 20 years seniority. These are high-level executives at large organizations with a lot of resources, so they're used to a very high level of quality in training and other materials. Attendees told us Leadership in Practice met or exceeded their expectations."

It fits with the association's strategy to grow membership without the limitations of physical location as well as the desire to continue conversations year-round and provide programming whenever members want it, wherever they may be, at whatever career stage.

When Programs and Activities Don't Fit

There are consequences of a product line (and by "product line" we mean the menu of programs, services, products, and activities the association offers) that lacks fit. They are:

Competitive Exposure

As Porter points out, free-standing and unintegrated services or businesses are easy for competitors to copy or attack. Different competitors can pick off services one at a time. Systems or integrated services or businesses are difficult to emulate or compete with.

When you hold out your hand with fingers extended, they will be easy to break. But if you clasp your hands together with your fingers intertwined, breaking one of the fingers is not so easy. It's a good analogy for how fit works.

Communication Challenges

Most will agree: Getting your association's message to the member and the marketplace is becoming more difficult by the day. The number of communication channels is growing. The number of players is increasing—all while the amount of time a member has to absorb media is decreasing.

Which is easier to communicate: a cohesive, well-coordinated set of offerings or a disjointed mishmash of stuff collected over the years? Positioning the association in the member's mind will be significantly enhanced with a product line that is related and integrated and makes sense. Members are not likely to take the time to dissect an uncoordinated, jumbled assortment of products and services to determine what might have value. Too many associations have a jungle of offerings; just look at how complex a typical association's website is. Then look at your competitors: Do they make your member work hard to find value in their offerings?

Organizational Complexity

A complex collection of unrelated programs and services creates organizational problems. Large organizations are likely to have silo structures where staff rarely, if ever, interact or communicate (much less collaborate). Their efforts and activities have no relationship to each other. In many instances, they are competitive rather than cooperative. In other situations, they vie for attention, priority, and resources. Where is the advantage in this scenario? Where is the synergy? How is this arrangement adding value to the member?

The organizational implications for a small association are enormous. With a staff of two or three (or even one!), each individual has to manage multiple programs, services, products, and activities having little in common with each other. Staff complete work on the insurance program, take off the insurance hat and put on the education hat. Two hours later, they take off the education hat and put on the community outreach committee liaison hat. It's more like a juggling act than a management function!

Consider just the down time between tasks. If each shift takes just 15 minutes to get reoriented and an average day involves five independent tasks, staff is spending more than six hours (or 15 percent of their time) a week just transitioning from one unrelated function to the other. In contrast, in an association with a tightly integrated service portfolio, this lost time is minimized. Transitioning from continuing education to certification to the program content committee liaison is not the same as the leap required to move from insurance to government relations to express delivery discounts.

Lack of program fit affects volunteer functioning as well. Committees can be as siloed as staff. The valuable volunteer human capital dispersed among many functions and activities without the benefit of integration spoils synergy. The cost for a small association is higher, as its dependence on volunteers is greater than in the larger association.

Human Capital Consequences

In small associations, managing diverse programs and services results in staff members who are jacks of all trades and masters of none. Though handling many tasks is an admirable skill, it's a competitive disadvantage with built-in inefficiencies. Think of two associations, both with a staff of five. One has an integrated portfolio of services with a high degree of fit. This staff looks like a basketball team: two guards, two forwards and a center. The other association is running five distinct businesses with little relationship among them. This staff has a hockey defenseman, a third baseman, a basketball player, a wide receiver, and a soccer goalie.

What does your staff look like? Are members of your staff playing on different fields or courts? Are they playing completely different games? Are they wearing different uniforms and using different equipment? If they are, you probably feel the downsides of not having fit.

CHAPTER SEVEN

Capitalizing on Fit

"Achieving fit is difficult because it requires the integration of decisions and actions across many subunits."
— Michael Porter[42]

An association's approach to achieving product and service integration and cohesion must be focused on its strengths. When defining your core theme or the underlying concept for your fit strategy, the first place you should go is to your strength. Designing your fit around anything but your strength is not likely to succeed, for all the reasons noted previously.

When considering programs and services, these questions help:

- Does this fit with our strength?
- Is this aligned with what we do best?
- Does it support the areas where we provide the highest value to our members?

For example, a trade association may have defined its primary strength or key competency as its ability to improve member company performance. Its core product is a robust source of industry information. It is the number-one resource for operating ratios, market share, sales by category, compensation, and other data that are critical to companies in the industry. Any new service or program has to fit with this strength. Seminars designed to facilitate use of the data fit. Consulting services capitalizing on the information fits. A mobile app that calculates company comparisons to industry averages fits. An insurance program doesn't fit. A jobs board doesn't fit. A shipping discount doesn't fit.

Let's say a professional society identifies its fundamental strength as improving the competence of its members. Its core services are educational seminars and conferences. All additional programs and services need to fit with professional development. A certification program fits. Personal professional assessment tools fit. Government advocacy doesn't fit. An insurance program doesn't fit. A credit card program doesn't fit. Abandoning the latter activities (especially if they are revenue generators), though not easy, is a necessary step on the road to relevance. We address abandoning programs in Chapter 10.

Don't Force Fit

Ultimately, the question of whether a program or service fits is a judgment. The evaluation requires thought, candor, honesty, and discipline. Association executives and leaders must anticipate the tendency for both staff and volunteers to contend that their idea, proposal, or new service fits. They will likely come up with a rationale, convoluted if necessary, to make a case that their new benefit is an enhancement to the integrated approach to the service portfolio. Ask the following questions to keep rogue programs from creeping into the benefit package and eroding your fit:

- What is the direct linkage of the new service to the association's core strength? How does it build on the strengths of existing activities?

- How does the proposed benefit complement or reinforce the other programs and products in our integrated service portfolio?

- How does the new offering improve the cohesive benefits package that currently exists?

Sometimes, articulating the answers to the above questions is enough to be able to talk yourself, staff member, or volunteers out of a program or service simply because fit isn't obvious. And when fit is not obvious, it doesn't exist.

Service Suites

While the ideal situation is a single theme with all services and programs aligned and integrated, it is unlikely that many associations can achieve this optimal position in the near term. Member usage, financial considerations, and tradition will all interfere. There is, however, a vehicle for associations to move in the right direction and capitalize on the benefits of fit: the service suite.

In essence, a service suite is set of programs and services within the association's assortment of programs and services that are integrated and reinforce each other. The best approach would be to build service suites around the association's strongest programs. It can also be a way to organize material for members, as many do around the competencies necessary for certification.

For example, the Independent Insurance Agents and Brokers of America (IIABA) is in the process of developing a suite of services and products to help its members use technology to enhance agency operational performance. The concept envisions software programs, educational offerings, consulting services, best practice benchmarking, and peer advisory councils—all designed to support agencies' use of technology. The various aspects of fit are obvious: benchmark data will support consulting services, which will generate educational opportunities, which will engage members who will be exposed to software tailored to their business. Further, the association has launched two major initiatives to enhance the competitiveness of members: a national consumer co-brand, Trusted Choice, which will provide local agencies with a national identity, and the Consumer Agent Portal (CAP), which offers search engine optimization, social media, and website development. While IIABA will continue to advocate member interests to government and carriers, it can now address a major emerging member needs while capitalizing on the power of fit.

The service suite is likely to have immediate application in many associations. Once the association recognizes the potential of the strategy, there may be existing programs and products that do, in fact, fit but have never been thought of in this context. Simply clustering them into a suite configuration and marketing them as a cohesive unit could have significant payoff.

The 3,000-member National Association of College Stores uses fit to organize its myriad product and service offerings in a way that makes sense for members. On the NACS website, "Tools and Resources" are organized into suites of service based on six competency domains of college store retailing. They include college store operations, course materials and intellectual property, and marketing and campus relations. In each of these areas, NACS offers a suite of services that includes practical templates, samples, kits, and guides. The easy-to-navigate structure leads to increased use of complementary services. A member finds a template he can use, and in the process learns of a related kit that he can use as well.

The Profitable Outlier Dilemma

What about the program or product that doesn't fit but makes money? Sometimes a lot of money, often so much that it subsidizes a great deal of the association's member benefits. At the extreme, what you have in some instances is a profitable product trying to be an association.

We specifically recall an association with a trade show that used to generate huge net profits. We say "used to" because the market changed and the party is over. The association spent most of its time trying to figure out what to do with the net proceeds that would have value to the members. After years of no success, they offered a conference in which they waived the registration fee for members and even gave them a cash payment to cover travel expenses! (We're not making this up.)

In this case, the profitable program "fits" the bottom line. It subsidized other programs that weren't capable of being offered profitably. Remember, one has to ask why the association offers programs that don't meet the market test of self-sustainability. If the product or service is so valuable, why isn't the member willing to pay for it? Why does it need a subsidy?

There are three options for the cash cow that creates money but doesn't fit.

1. Discontinue the program either by phasing it out or selling it. This was the approach taken by Pfizer executives when they realized some products no longer fit their strategy, as Paul Leinwand and Cesare Mainardi wrote about in the June 2010 issue of *Harvard Business Review*:

> Thanks to the acquisition of Warner-Lambert, the consumer health care portfolio had migrated away from over-the-counter drugs and into personal care (Schick razors and shaving cream) and confectionary (Chiclets, Trident, and Bubblicious gums)—categories that leveraged distinctly different capability sets. Personal care requires specific innovation in skin technologies, keeping up with fashion trends, and the ability to design attractive packaging. Confectionary requires rapid cycle flavor innovation and the ability to command space at the front of the store near the cash register. If Pfizer no longer was going to invest in those capabilities, it needed to divest those products or risk strategic incoherence.
>
> In 2003, Pfizer sold the confectionary products business to Cadbury Schweppes and the Schick–Wilkinson Sword wet-shave business to Energizer Holdings. These divestitures enabled Pfizer to focus even more attention and resources on growing its global health care brands (Listerine, Zyrtec, and Nicorette) at above-market rates and acquiring new brands....
>
> By 2006, Pfizer Consumer Healthcare had grown its business to nearly $4 billion in annual sales and was a premier company in its category, delivering a rate of growth double the industry average.[43]

2. Spin it off to another organization with a residual worked into the deal that will provide an ongoing revenue stream without cluttering up your service portfolio. This way, members still have access to the program or service. The association cleans up its portfolio, jettisoning the product. And a revenue stream, although perhaps not equal to what was previously enjoyed, is preserved.

This option was selected by the Texas Trial Lawyers Association (TTLA) for TrialSmith®, its service that started as an online deposition database and has grown to include a social network, jury reports, and daily legal news. TrialSmith® is now a separate, for-profit corporation that pays a rebate to participating associations and litigation groups based on the percentage of services used by their respective members. In 2011, more than 128 organizations received rebates totaling $879,000, including TTLA, which received $42,159 from TrialSmith®.[44]

3. Continue to run the program and use the net revenue not just to subsidize other programs but to nurture them to profitability. Over time, wean them from the subsidy, gradually improving the financial performance to the point where the subsidy is not required and they can stand on their own. And if it becomes obvious that a program simply can't command the price it costs to produce it, ultimately you either have to reduce the costs associated with its production or discontinue it. The challenge here is to balance the use of the net revenue generated. If you don't reinvest in the "cash cow," its performance will eventually deteriorate.

Technology Fit

One valuable byproduct of fit, whether it encompasses the association's entire program and service platform or follows the suite of services concept, is the important guidance it provides you for technology planning. Your overall fit strategy needs a technology fit complement. If you do not aggressively capitalize on technology in delivering value in the core area where you are integrating services and interlocking activities, you are on the fast track to irrelevance.

Too often associations fall into the trap of adopting technology applications without a clear understanding of how they will add value. They frequently jump on the technology of the day. This results in owning technologies in search of a purpose. The theme or focus of your fit will help answer the important question of where and how technology might add value.

For example, the individual membership association with a career focus can ask: How can we exploit distance learning? What are the best models for eLearning? How can we maximize a job board? Can we use Facebook to connect with students? Once the list of possibilities is developed, priorities can be established and you can get to work knowing that you are appropriately investing time and effort—and that these technology efforts align with your overall fit decisions.

The trade association with a government relations focus can ask: What is the best database system to mobilize members on advocacy issues? Can we use text messaging to raise PAC contributions? Does Twitter have potential for communicating with legislators and their staff? Would issue-specific Facebook pages improve our effectiveness? The answers to these questions will give valuable guidance to critical technology investments aligned with your core business.

Governance Fit

One final dimension of fit for associations is governance. While not "fit" in the traditional strategic sense, it is of critical importance for associations that want to achieve exceptional performance in the future.

Boards, in particular, have to fit with the association's strategic intentions. It's no longer sufficient to send a popular member from a district or region as a delegate to serve on the association's board. Nominating committees (though we prefer calling them leadership development committees because this suggests a more comprehensive approach to identifying and preparing leaders) should no longer be asking, "Whom can we get to serve?" Instead they should be carefully identifying, vetting, and grooming potential leaders. Today's boards have to be composed purposefully if associations are to remain both relevant and competitive. Thought must be given to what competencies, qualities, and attributes association volunteers need to govern (defined "direct and control") the association effectively.

Politically charged, ego-based, geographic, and/or special-interest board composition simply does not contribute to performance. In fact, it can be a major hindrance and diversion of resources. The challenging environment is unkind to associations whose boards do not recognize and respond to this new normal. Leaders must have discipline. They must understand the critical importance of intelligent resource allocation. They must understand the imperative of clear focus. They must be comfortable with the inevitable tradeoffs involved. They must ask the critical question, "Does this new idea fit our core theme or focus?" And they have to be able to say no when appropriate.

Finding Fit

The days of associations' being able to exist with diverse and unrelated services and activities are quickly coming to an end. The association's product line must fit and be integrated with offerings that complement and reinforce each other. Competitors with a single focus will outperform an association offering multiple lines of services and activities, particularly when they are not related and integrated. Time-pressed members with instant access to scores of options will gravitate to sources that excel. The cluttered communication environment will be unkind to attempts to promote multifaceted offerings. The complexity of managing a mixed bag of dissimilar products and services will hobble the association's execution and use valuable resources.

Fit may be more difficult to identify than strengths. Fit is a relatively new concept in the association community. Start by identifying a unifying theme for your organization. These categories may be a good starting point:

- Government (lobbying, legislative updates, grassroots activity, campaign support, regulatory compliance)

- Market assistance (helping members be competitive in the market)

- Careers (professional development, job boards, certification, compensation studies)

- Competence (continuing education, scholarly journals, online networks, scholarship programs)

Once you've identified a theme, take stock of your current inventory of programs, products, services, and activities and give your association a "fit rating" using a scale of 1 to 5, where 1 means little or no fit, 2 means poor fit, 3 means some fit, 4 means good fit, 5 means excellent fit. Like the matrices in *Race for Relevance*, this exercise is designed to be enlightening and to stimulate conversation. It also helps to illustrate to staff and leaders what you mean when you talk about fit and how it helps or hinders the association. Once you know what fits, you can decide what to do with elements that don't fit, including discontinuing or selling them, spinning them off to another organization, or continuing to run the program to help nurture other programs to profitability.

As you're rating services for fit, consider your strengths. Programs and services that fit to strength should receive the bulk of your time, attention, and energy.

Finally, be willing to eliminate the misfits. In *Race for Relevance,* we suggested evaluating the performance of all your services and activities, possibly discontinuing underperformers. We are more convinced than ever this is a critical activity. Now, however, we're suggesting you take a look at the remaining menu of services, this time evaluating them on fit rather than performance. We believe the exercise will be both beneficial and enlightening.

Role of the CEO

As with the other strategies, the CEO should play a large role as the "keeper of fit," since he or she has the deepest understanding and knowledge of all the association's offerings. As new programs are considered, the CEO should weigh in regarding how they fit with other activities, perhaps grading their fitness. The CEO also can be helpful in providing input regarding staff fit—or how the addition of an employee works with current staff expertise. When fit isn't present, the board and executive committee should know what the ramifications are for the association. Finally, The CEO should be given permission to ask, "How does this fit?" when he or she senses the board is wandering or when there's not a close fit with a new program or service offering.

Another way the CEO can be helpful is by integrating "fit criteria" into strategic planning. Strategic objectives or initiatives have to be aligned with the fit concept and direction and institutionalized in the planning process. This may require work before a planning session to identify and articulate the unifying concept for approval prior to a planning retreat. Thoughtful advance work helps ensure the board has the information it needs to make informed decisions regarding long-range planning.

Role of the Board

Of all the strategies in this book, fit may be the most difficult for the board to grasp, since it may be a new concept for volunteer leaders. The board would be wise to articulate strength and identify a unifying theme for the organization to more easily measure fit in the future. Identifying a theme may not be easy, especially for the association used to being all things to all people and providing a wide variety of benefits to offer something for everyone. If the board doesn't have the energy or inclination to go back and make fit determinations about current programs and services, at the minimum it should agree to do so going forward. This task is easier when a concentration decision has been made.

Repeatedly, in our conversations with CEOs, we hear them say, "I don't need a bunch of yes people on the board. What I really need is individuals who will help me thoughtfully work through all the strategy decisions required on a regular basis." The board can be an asset to both the association and the CEO when it is willing to engage in constructive debate and discussion with the goal of developing clarity and consensus. This means being willing to wade into uncertain areas, such as what fit really means and how it can affect the association going forward. We find these types of conversations can be energizing and they often contribute to building a more productive relationship between the board and CEO.

Case Study

Taking it to the Streets: Telling the Story of Metal

ASSOCIATION: Metal Construction Association (MCA)

BUDGET: $1.8 million

NUMBER OF STAFF MEMBERS: 12, managed by the Association Management Center (an association management company)

NUMBER OF MEMBERS: 90 companies

MCA was born 30 years ago in response to a negative image of the metal construction industry. According to Susan Wallace, who wrote about MCA for *Forum* magazine, "Individual member companies were combating a 'rusty barn' perception and realized an industry-wide effort would work better to spread the good news about the durability and sustainability of metal."[45] Since then, every effort has been designed to get more metal on buildings. This mission creates fit for the association.

Today, the association works on behalf of members to eliminate barriers to metal use in construction by monitoring and responding to codes and regulations that affect metal, supporting product performance testing, and initiating research.

One aspect of the initiative is "heavy hitter" meetings sponsored by the association that bring together facility managers, architects, and cost analysts to teach them how metal helps both the bottom line and building appearance. So far, the association has convened 30 such meetings. The initiative is committed to communicating metal's advantages in lifespan, energy efficiency, and fire resistance.

Though the initiative was created with funding from outside the association and initially supported only by some members, a change in sponsorship due to the tough economy prompted a change. Supporting the program is now mandatory for members through dues. Despite the change, the association added seven members in 2010.

According to a 2010 study by FMI Corp., since 2006 the use of metal in commercial and institutional roofing and wall construction has increased around 20 percent.[46]

Staying the course in promoting metal use hasn't been easy, says Mark Engle, principal of the Association Management Center, the firm that manages the association. "We were ruthless about grounding our discussions. If something brought up in a meeting was interesting, but didn't increase the use of metal, we moved on."[47]

Fit takes discipline. But it also produces results. Members see the value of the program, whether it's in industry statistics or in their own bottom line. Dick Bus, who served on the MCA board for 19 years, went to a heavy-hitter meeting with Fairfax, Virginia, County Public Schools (the 11th largest district in the country) and ended up working with them on two projects. Is this a return on investment for member dues? Absolutely. It's also a "return on fit (ROF)" for the association.

What's your ROF?

CHAPTER EIGHT

The Lean Association: Aligning People and Processes Efficiently

"Continuous improvement is not about the things you do well—that's work. Continuous improvement is about removing the things that get in the way of your work. The headaches, the things that slow you down, that's what continuous improvement is all about."

– Bruce Hamilton[48]

The competitive association cannot afford to be inefficient. It cannot misuse or squander resources in ways that don't add value. Like elite athletes, associations are going to have to be in top shape and perform with maximum efficiency to ensure a success and relevancy in the future.

When outlining the components of a sustainable competitive advantage, Michael Porter, writing in the *Harvard Business Review*[49] said efficient processes and quality improvement methods are essential fundamentals for a competitive organization. Thus, operational effectiveness is not a differentiator; it is a basic requirement just to get in the game.

Operational excellence may be a given in the business environment, but it is often a stranger in the association community. Many associations have been so focused on member services or the value proposition that they haven't had time to assess operational effectiveness. Consequently, it is a powerful strategy when applied to the not-for-profit world.

When it comes to operational effectiveness in associations, we have four observations:

1. There is general complacency with existing approaches to performing the association's work. Meetings are produced essentially the same way as they have been for years. Committees operate the same way as in the past. Boards function essentially the same way they have for decades. Systematically analyzing the association's processes and continuously identifying opportunities to improve output or increase efficiency is rare. Associations appear to be captives of "that's the way we've always done it" thinking.

2. There is a lot of waste in associations. Wasted resources. Wasted time. Wasted effort. Wasted human capital. Wasted opportunities. This is not malicious waste. It is simply a product of being bound by tradition. There's been little economic pressure to improve efficiency and eliminate waste—until now. Competitive pressures and resource constraints leave little tolerance for efforts and resources inefficiently allocated to programs, activities, and other outputs. Increasing financial pressure and reduced staff resources create a mandate for greater operational efficiency.

3. Little thought is given to methodically driving down operating costs. The prevailing thinking is that over time, as operating costs increase because of inflation or other reasons, the association will simply raise dues to cover them. Other than the occasional budget-cutting exercise—usually a reaction to difficult economic conditions or poor financial performance—few associations are consciously and purposefully working to reduce their costs. There is a big difference between budget cutting and operational excellence. One is a reaction; the other is a way of thinking.

To illustrate the mindset, how many times have you heard an association executive or leader mention "the last time we raised dues"? Usually it's accompanied by an eye roll and a story about how difficult it was to pass the initiative—even for as little as a $3 increase! And how many times have you heard staff or a leader mention "our initiative to reduce operating costs"? Associations tend to be more focused on member services and providing member value than on operational excellence. But the two are not mutually exclusive.

4. Operational initiatives usually die of neglect. The average association executive is extremely busy. Between managing the association governance structure, annual calendar, and the bottom line, most don't have extra time to manage additional projects. And when they do, the proposals are often association leaders' pet projects or "emergency" programs designed to protect members or their reputations. Rarely are they programs designed to strengthen the association itself. When they are, they are often initiated but forgotten with the next crisis or cast aside with the advent of a new program or service. And it doesn't help that the board rarely takes an interest in or supports efforts to improve operational performance.

So many associations are overweight and out of shape. They haven't watched their diet and they don't exercise. Yet today's intensely competitive marketplace requires an organization to be healthy, increasingly efficient, and highly productive. In a word, tomorrow's association must be lean.

History of Efficiency Initiatives

Improving operational efficiency and productivity is not new. Benjamin Franklin's *Poor Richard's Almanac* exhorted Colonials in the 1700s to avoid unnecessary costs and to economize. In the late 1800s and early 1900s Frederick Taylor was regarded as the pioneer of "scientific management," which sought to systematically analyze work and identify opportunities to improve productivity through planning and training. In 1913, Henry Ford introduced moving assembly lines in his factories, resulting in tremendous improvements in productivity. Toyota's Chief Engineer, Taiichi Ohno, is recognized as the founder of the Toyota Production System, which popularized the concepts of waste elimination and flow improvement to enhance performance and introduced "Just in Time" manufacturing processes to reduce inventory. W. Edwards Deming, the father of Total Quality Management (TQM), focused on continuous improvement of processes and outputs.

In the 1960s and 1970s, increased global competition resulted in an intense focus on costs. Tasks included determining the true costs of production, identifying methods to decrease costs, analyzing competitors' costs, and projecting cost improvements with increases in volume. This was an environment dominated by the low-cost producer strategy. The essential elements of strategy were "costs, customers, and competition."[50] Associations did not participate in this cost movement; they actually went in the opposite direction. They let their costs grow at will and simply raised their prices (dues).

Managing and reducing costs must now be an essential strategy for associations because of the third c: competition. While it may seem curious that associations did not participate earlier in this movement, the indifference can be easily explained. The competitive environment had not yet arrived for membership organizations as it had for businesses. But now that day has come.

Waste and Value

Lean manufacturing or lean production refers to practices that maintain or improve value with less effort or work. In lean thinking, waste is anything that does not contribute to value. This view of waste takes some time to sink in. Any activity that consumes time, resources, or space but does not add value to the end product, service, or activity is considered waste.

What Has Value?

The first step in adopting lean thinking is to define value. (Are you seeing the thread here? So far we've advocated focusing on strength, concentrating resources, and fit. All are designed to create the human and financial resources to produce a stellar member value proposition—one that's not mediocre or "ho-hum" but that's so strong it's a "must have" for members in your market.) Defining value is not easy for association executives and even more challenging for association leadership because it's not the way things have always been done.

Member value can be elusive and is often intangible, making it difficult to see. Further, according to Jaynie L. Smith, author of *Creating Competitive Advantage*, "… a competitive advantage is rarely unique and not often sustainable over an extended period of time."[51] Thus, it can be a moving target (albeit a slow moving one).

When thinking about value, consider Sarah Sladek's advice from *The End of Membership as We Know It:*

> Members join your association because they believe in your ability to help them solve a problem for them. They renew their membership when you are successful at solving the problem, engage them in a community, and make them feel good about being a member. So a successful membership benefits formula is equally practical and emotional.[52]

The following helps when considering value:

Members decide what has value. Not the board. Not the staff. Not a committee. The members. Too often boards and staff assume they know what members value. This is a chancy assumption. Smith calls it "dangerous disparity." In *Creating Competitive Advantage,* she shares a story about the Visiting Nurse Association of Florida (VNA), which supplies health care services to the homebound, including skilled nursing care and therapy, patient education, and community and social services. VNA managers identified the association's nonprofit status as a competitive advantage. However, customer research with two different groups told a different story. Smith says, "We soon discovered that dangerous disparity was rearing its ugly head. The staff members were way off in guessing which attributes were most important to each market.... Topping the list of *least important* attributes on both surveys was—you guessed it—not-for-profit status."[53] VNA broke company records by increasing revenues 40 percent after it started a new campaign touting its competitive advantages rather than its nonprofit status. That's the power of accurately identifying value.

Value is validated by a member's willingness to exchange money or time for something. If it's not worth money or time, it doesn't have value. Isn't it interesting that people refer to both time and money as a currency: how we *spend* our time and money and where we *spend* it? We think currency, something that is used as a medium of exchange, is a key element in the value equation. When members don't want to invest time and money, there's a value vacuum—or an awareness problem.

When membership declines, associations should ask why former members no longer think the association is worth a dues check. And when attendance at the annual conference starts trending downward, they should ask why members don't think the annual conference is worth the cost of registration and the time spent away from work or family. When possible, formal research should be conducted to codify the real answer— not just what staff or volunteers think. Too often conjecture and hunches drive responses.

"Some value" creates a conundrum for an association. Think about attendance at a meeting that has been declining for years but still has value for a modest number of members. A program that is used by a handful of members also has some value. An argument could be made that everything an association offers has some value. It is easier and more politically expedient to set the bar low by assigning some value to every-thing, thereby maintaining activities and services with little value rather than focusing solely on those with the highest value.

In today's competitive environment, an association is not likely to perform well with loose, substandard definitions of value. Members are well informed and have high expectations. These high expectations are a poor match with an association's menu of programs or services that have only some value.

Associations must be more rigorous in defining value. They must set higher standards for programs and services. They must challenge the value of offerings that do not attract takers. They must address the incon-venient lack of attendees for their meetings. We frequently hear staff and volunteers kid themselves about the value of meetings or services when attendance or use is low. "The members who attend think the meeting is terrific; it gets good ratings. But attendance is dismal." Or, "The companies that use the service are very happy with it. Unfortunately it is only three percent of the membership."

Assessing value requires consciously thinking through the threshold question, "What is the minimum percentage of our members that must use a program to validate its value and to continue offering it?" If only five percent of our members attend our most significant meeting, what is that telling us? Does it really have the value that we believe it does?

Of course, related to the threshold question is the issue of cost and return. What if only five percent of our members are using it, but it is a viable, profitable (yes, with all overhead costs allocated to it!) program? The marketplace is telling us that this has value. So threshold thinking has to take into account economic performance, and decision makers must exercise judgment.

To remain competitive, associations must quit making excuses. "If nonmembers knew what we're doing in government relations, they'd see the value and join." Or, "It's a great program, members just don't know about it."

Value changes. Adrian J. Slywotzky introduced the concept of "value migration" in the book *Value Migration: How to Think Several Moves Ahead of the Competition.*[54] Value migrates from outdated business models to those that better meet customer needs. Often technological advances are a factor. Horse and buggy to automobile. Travel agent to online ticketing. Associations have seen value migrate from networking breaks at a conference to 24/7 social media, from print publications to digital publications, and from classroom learning to distance learning. When changes are rapidly adopted by competitors, associations are at a competitive disadvantage because they are generally slow in decision making and often cater to late adopters.

One way of determining value is to use the six attributes of customer value as defined by James P. Womack and Daniel T. Jones in their book, *Lean Solutions: How Companies and Customers Can Create Value and Wealth Together.*[55] The authors suggest that value is created by the following:

1. **Complete problem solution.** Here the association defines the member's challenge or opportunity and provides a total solution, eliminating the need to go to another source. The "suites of service" concept we discussed in the previous chapter is a way of creating value here. But be careful. "Complete" solutions take resources and you can get stretched thin. They may also require prolonged access to specific expertise, which may or may not be readily available.

2. **Efficient solution.** The association fulfills a need without wasting the member's time. The transaction is quick and easy. An example is continuing education tracking for professionals who need to take

a mandated number of hours in a given time. The association offers a system that keeps track of the continuing education hours, so members know where they stand and what courses they need to take to remain in compliance.

3. **What I want.** Associations must provide solutions to members exactly how they want it, not how the association is set up to deliver it. For example, the association has a printed directory, but members want to be able to access an email address on their smart phone. We know of an association that returned to a printed directory from an online version. Now the directory is more likely to be out-of-date, and members can't easily search or click on a link to call or email.

4. **Where I want it.** Where does the member need value? With mobile technology, this is rapidly becoming anywhere in the world. Don't underestimate this demand. According to the Mobile Marketing Association of Asia, out of the 6 billion people on the planet, 4.8 billion have a mobile device and only 4.2 billion own a toothbrush.[56]

5. **When I want it.** The priority must be not when the association wants to deliver a program or service but when the member needs it. Think about traditional annual educational conferences versus on-demand e-learning or the ability to access frequently asked questions any time of day or night on the internet.

6. **Make it simple.** Don't complicate the process. We've seen some very complex member services and difficult-to-complete membership applications in our work, including one that required signatures of current members and two consecutive readings of the prospective member's name at the monthly meeting. If your name was read at a spring meeting before the summer break, that meant starting the reading process over in the fall—and often a delay of six months or more before membership was granted. (No, we're not making this up!) We've also seen tripartite (where members join local, state, and national simultaneously) or federated organizations that require a different application for each level of membership rather than using one universal member application.

Now that we've taken a closer look at member value—what it is and how we create it—we can turn to how to achieve lean operations. Remember, the purpose of operating lean is to be operationally effective so that resources are used wisely to create or add to member value. Anything else is reengineering your association for the wrong reason.

CHAPTER NINE

Understanding and Reducing Waste

*"There is nothing so useless as doing efficiently
that which should not be done at all."*
– PETER DRUCKER[57]

To date, the lean movement has been applied primarily in manufacturing. It has a very manufacturing-oriented perspective, some of which is difficult to translate to service organizations. Yet interestingly, "although lean production is usually seen as a manufacturing concept, many of its tools were developed in the service industry."[58]

Lean approaches are being adopted in areas as diverse as call centers, higher education, and software development. Even entrepreneurs are getting involved. Eric Ries' *The Lean Startup: How Today's Entrepreneurs Use Continuous Innovation to Create Radically Successful Businesses* is a *New York Times* bestseller.[59]

Adapting lean concepts requires another level of adjustment for the association community. But stick with us as we walk through this. It will change the way you think about resources and how they can be optimized.

Seven Wastes

The "seven wastes" was a way of categorizing waste in manufacturing by Toyota's Chief Engineer, Taiichi Ohno.[60] The fundamental concept involves eliminating activities or resources that do not add value. It is a way of thinking, and not everything is applicable to associations. You'll see that a lot is, however:

1. Overproduction

Essentially, overproduction is manufacturing an item before it is needed. Overproduction is considered the worst type of waste as it results in other types of waste that follow: inventory, waiting, and defects.

Think about all the copies of that book you published last year that have gone unsold or the copies of the standards that you overprinted that are in storage. Addressing overproduction resulted in "Just in Time" (JIT) processes. For an association, on-demand printing is the JIT equivalent solution for that storeroom full of books and publications that you may own. And carefully tracking projected versus actual demand for products and services increases future accuracy when placing product and printing orders.

2. Waiting

Whenever something is not moving or being processed, the waste of waiting occurs. In manufacturing, it was found that a very high percentage (in some cases, 99 percent!) of a product's life was spent waiting to be processed. A lot of a program or service's life in associations can be spent waiting—waiting for the next committee or task force meeting, waiting for board action, or waiting for review, proofing, or approval. Think about a program or service that you initiated recently. How much time did it sit idle as it waited to move through the approval process—and how long did it take to get through production as a result?

3. Transportation

In the manufacturing process, when a product or part is in transit it is not adding value. There is a small element of transportation in associations; for example, think about travel to a conference or to meetings with members. The time spent in transportation (cabs, airport, flight, etc.) is actually waste. The only thing that really adds value is being at the conference or the meeting. Another example is shuttles from the hotel to the convention center. Your members' time spent in shuttles is waste; being at the convention is what has value. Consider this when making site visits. Time is especially important when your members are self-employed. Days out of the office can mean a reduction in income and comes into play for members when deciding whether to attend meetings. Wasted time should be minimized.

4. Motion

This waste refers to worker ergonomics like unnecessary bending, lifting, and walking. Excessive motion is waste and has health and safety implications. This sounds like a manufacturing-only type of waste. But it comes into play when gathering inventory to deliver to members, getting to and from storage areas, or accessing any type of hard files (as opposed to those stored online).

5. Inventory

In manufacturing, raw materials, work in progress, and finished product that has not been delivered are considered waste. Inventory is basically a product of overproduction or waiting. Association inventory ranges from membership certificates or cards waiting to be shipped to books and other learning tools waiting to be sold to unused member directories sitting in storage.

We would also argue that association reserves are a kind of inventory. Reserves represent an association's financial resources that are not being delivered or converted to value for the member. Assets that do not add value are waste. Thus, an overabundance of reserves is waste.

6. Overprocessing

It is waste when more work is done on a product than is required by the customer. How often has association staff overdone an event or service at a conference because a board member thought it was important, but it turned out that the members really didn't care, or how much staff time and effort goes into magazine graphics and formats when the member just wants quick information?

7. Defects

Waste occurs when defects in product quality require rework or products end up on the scrap pile. Think of the committee recommendation that the board sends back for modification or the committee whose output is of no value. That is a defect. Other examples might include a staff proposal that was not thoroughly thought through and the board requests it be reworked, an educational seminar that attracts only 10 percent of what was projected, or a publication that lays an egg. One of the problems in associations is that rarely do they scrap these offerings. They just let them limp along. And resources are allocated to things that don't have value or result in that pesky "some value" category.

The Eighth Waste

As lean thinking evolved and expanded beyond manufacturing, an eighth waste emerged: the waste of human capital. W. Edwards Deming wrote, "The greatest waste in America is failure to use the abilities of people."[61]

This eighth area of waste is the most applicable to trade associations, professional societies, and other tax-exempt organizations. And in our opinion, it is the most important to address for four reasons.

First, most associations identify their human capital as their most significant strength. This generally includes both the volunteer leadership and staff. Volunteers bring considerable insight and expertise, often cutting-edge, in their profession or industry. The staff complements this with management and functional skills and increasingly professional or industry knowledge. Organizations (particularly service organizations) that waste their most valuable resource are going to underperform against those that optimize their human resources.

Second, associations and other nonprofits are people intensive. According to ASAE's *Operating Ratio Report, 14th Edition,* 37.2 percent of the average association's operating costs are for salaries and related personnel expenses.[62] Further, the commitment of time and knowledge of boards, committees, and task forces is considerable. Then add the volunteers who participate in lobbying activity, write articles, develop standards, prepare and present educational programs, and on and on.

These are huge resources. And yet we waste a lot of them by not coordinating efforts, ignoring (or not setting) deadlines, not setting clear goals or expectations, or assigning work and not communicating when the parameters change.

Third, many associations are small and their human capital is precious. With one or two paid staff, such organizations rely heavily on volunteers. In the association community, the small association can least afford to waste its limited human capital. But unfortunately, many do.

Finally, increased time pressures in our society today make getting committed volunteers harder and harder. In our opinion, one of the primary reasons that members decline volunteer positions (or stop volunteering once they start) is because they don't see it as a good use of their time. They won't waste their time. They simply won't sign up, or they'll stop showing up if they don't feel that their time and talent is being used well. Some refuse leadership roles for the same reason.

Analyzing the waste of an association's human resources is fairly straightforward. It happens in three ways:

- Underoptimization: not using the human capital to its full potential.

- Improper utilization: using the human capital for work that has no value and should not be done or should be done by staff rather than volunteers.

- No utilization: leaving the human capital idle.

The micromanaging board is the most egregious form of underoptimization. Here you generally have a group of highly intelligent people, often with advanced degrees, decades of experience, and rare levels of expertise and knowledge, spending time talking about what city should host a conference, whether the directory should be printed or digital, or what media is best for an association initiative. It is a flagrant waste of human capital because it not only underoptimizes the board, it underoptimizes the time and talent of the most valuable staff: the CEO.

Associations are particularly prone to allocating the human resource to activities or functions that shouldn't be done in the first place, often supporting marginal programs or services, sometimes because a single board member passionately appeals for its continuation. Supporting activities that serve a fraction of the membership, that are the "right thing to do," or that are done because "that's what associations are supposed to do," can be a major source of inefficiency.

There is another, lower profile situation when an association has people potential but doesn't use it at all. A great example of this has been recently illuminated by Susan Cane's best-selling book, *Quiet: The Power of Introverts in a World That Can't Stop Talking.*[63] It makes the case that introverts in an organization are underused and are overpowered by high-profile extroverts.

ASAE's *The Decision to Join*[64] showed that board and committee members placed significantly higher importance on networking than did the average member. This would lead us to the conclusion, not surprisingly, that we disproportionately attract extroverts to association leadership positions. Where are the introverts? They are often unrepresented, leaving valuable human capital on the sidelines. And when they are involved, their opinions and perspectives can be drowned out by more vocal extroverts.

If associations are going to tap into this resource pool, they are going to have to use untraditional means to attract volunteers. For example, instead of choosing board members from those high-profile individuals who attend meetings and participate in committees, the association will need outreach methods to identify and recruit qualified, talented individuals who don't use those avenues to gain information and learn. This is where a leadership development committee (as opposed to a nominating committee) comes into play. We know there will be risks with members who are unknown quantities, but we believe the considerable untapped potential outweighs the downsides.

Other areas of waste include CEOs' spending time needlessly informing officers or the chair of day-to-day issues, CEO and association managers' attending meetings and not participating, and committee meetings that don't produce recommendations. Only the meeting that results in an approved or finalized recommendation has value.

Redundancies

Another area of waste is in redundant systems. The best example of redundant systems is component or constituent associations in a federated structure. Many national associations, particularly individual membership organizations, have related regional, state, or local associations. The relationships between the component associations and the national organization differ. Sometimes there are closely linked chapters with shared memberships and integrated dues. Others are totally independent, often competing for members and nondues revenue. But they are all are serving the same members and providing similar services. They each have systems that serve essentially the same functions: finance, dues billing, accounting, website, database, social media, conference and event planning, and other "back office" functions. Each of these functions requires equipment, software, human resources, office space, maintenance, and other support. These duplicative systems are not adding value and result in waste.

If you were designing a national structure with 50 state organizations, would you have 50 different databases, 50 different accounting systems, 50 different technology platforms? We think not. Think of the operating efficiencies, buying power leverage, and quality enhancements of a single "shared services" system. Of course, there would be costs and tradeoffs in the transition, but we did some quick math using ASAE's operating ratios.

For the average association, overhead accounts for 12 percent, according to ASAE's 2012 *Benchmarking in Association Management: Financial Operations Policies and Procedures (Volume 6)*.[65] With the average annual expenditures for a state association being $800,000, then overhead represents $96,000 of expenses annually. We believe that by sharing back office systems, the cost to each association would be reduced by 50 percent. Remember, it's not just equipment and systems; it's people and overhead as well. With that assumption, each state association could reduce its annual expenses by $48,000. For a 50-state federation, this converts to $2,400,000 a year of waste, totaling $12,000,000 over five years!

Consolidating overhead expenses represents an opportunity especially for tripartite and federated organizations at the national level. Service to constituencies can be strengthened and streamlined and redundancies eliminated. In this case, national adds both value and relevance to the state and local while strengthening all levels of the organization.

The Association for Corporate Growth (ACG Global) has tackled the issue of redundancies by building a robust suite of services to support and reduce burdens on its 58 chapters so that they can put their energy, creativity, and focus on delivering what matters most to more than 14,000 members: providing networking opportunities.

To reduce the considerable redundant functions that can create significant waste in a chapter system, ACG's global headquarters provides a range of administrative, back-office, and consultative services. These include:

- A master website with customizable chapter portals;
- An app platform that chapters can tailor;
- Online event registration and payment systems;
- Membership database and broadcast email services;
- Member dues invoiced and collected by ACG Global, with the chapter portion of dues rebated to chapters every two weeks;
- Chapter boards and volunteers covered under a master directors and officers policy as well as a general liability policy;
- Model bylaws and policies, along with a large database of samples, forms, and program ideas;
- Domain name registration, trademark registration, and a visual identity standards manual for all ACG Global logos and marks;
- Staff payroll and benefits processed for some full-time chapter staff, removing a major administrative burden from these chapters;
- Staffing to assist chapters in emergency situations, such as an unexpected vacancy in chapter staffing;
- Group tax filing (for United States chapters) and annual state corporation filings;
- Free consulting in strategic planning, membership development, board retreats, and other advisory services; and

• Access to $50,000 annually to support innovative chapter projects and $15,000 in matching funds for professional development of chapter staff.

ACG Global's approach is a good example for other federated associations. The concept is win-win: redundancies and costs are reduced; local activities are facilitated; and importantly, volunteers are supported administratively. If you haven't carefully considered this concept for your organization, you should.

Executive Committee/Board of Directors Redundancies

Another waste resulting from redundancy is inherent in executive committee and board of directors functioning. And it is a colossal waste, squandering the association's most precious human capital, the CEO and volunteer leaders. The executive committee often convenes for a meeting the day before the board meeting. They review the agenda items; examine the association's finances, membership, and meeting attendance figures; discuss the issues of the day; and make decisions to present to the board the next day.

The board then meets to review association's finances, membership, and meeting attendance figures; discuss the issues of the day; and react to (actually "ratify" is the more appropriate word) the executive committee decisions (often called "recommendations").

The board meeting is 90 percent repetition for the executive committee members and the CEO. Rare is the occasion when the board seriously challenges the executive committee's decisions or recommendations. The board meeting can be as much as 90 percent passive review by the directors. And it is a monumental waste, as the following analysis shows.

According to ASAE's website, in 2009, there were 90,908 trade and professional associations. Let's say 75 percent of them operate with an executive committee, even though it is probably higher than that. Let's say the average size of the board is 16 and it meets three times a year for one day. (According to the BoardSource Nonprofit Governance Index 2010, the average size of a board is 16 members.)[66] The average association board and CEO spend 408 hours a year in the boardroom (17 people times eight hours). Using our estimate, the 68,181 associations with executive committees spend almost 28 million wasted hours in meetings every year!

The lean association should adhere to the admonition of Eric Ries: "Most of all, we should stop wasting people's time."[67] Where is human capital being wasted in your organization?

Process Improvement

The following four steps are the keys to eliminating waste and maximizing the association's resources.

1. Define value for the member today. This requires internal analysis, member feedback, challenging long-held assumptions, asking a lot of questions, and accepting that what members value may have changed over the past couple of years. It will require honest answers and the courage to act on what you learn. And sometimes, it will require helping members figure out what's valuable in a changing marketplace.

For example, the Affordable Care Act resulted in significant shifts in medicine, including that it's getting more difficult for physicians to survive outside of group practices. Yet most medical societies are created to serve solo practitioners. As medical societies wrestle with this implication, they are also trying to help members figure out how to survive in an uncertain environment. We've been at many medical meetings and heard the words, "We don't know what this really means," as various aspects of the Affordable Care Act are dissected and discussed.

Though uncomfortable, uncertainty represents opportunity. According to Bill Mallon, senior director, strategy and innovation development for the Association of American Medical Colleges, his organization started to focus on process excellence because of an intentional push by the board and CEO to better position the association to respond to members' challenges resulting from changes in the healthcare environment. He notes, "The 2010 Affordable Care Act has major impacts for our members.... We realized we had to be better positioned to help our members tackle their biggest challenges. That meant we needed to do new things." To launch the new projects, the board approved the creation of a $5 million strategic investment fund for fiscal year 2011. To fund this strategic shift, the association had to look for ways to stop doing some things that weren't adding the same amount of value. This initiative is an excellent example of two things: identifying value today and using process improvement to help find the necessary resources to create and/or support value.

2. Identify all the steps required to get from concept to delivery of a program, service, or activity that has member value. In lean terminology, this is referred to as "value stream mapping." Drawing a diagram of all the steps that occur in the life of the product is almost always illuminating. Processes are often more complex than thought, with more steps along the stream than were apparent. And one phenomenon we often have seen when groups undertake this task is immediate agreement on where the waste and bottlenecks occur!

3. Remove or improve any steps in the process that do not add value to the final product. The one benefit of mapping is that it will almost always identify one or two major opportunities to eliminate waste or accelerate the process. According to Womack and Jones, "Indeed, the amount of human effort, time, space, tools, and inventories needed to design and provide a given service or good can typically be *cut in half* very quickly."[68] This quick return for the initial effort validates the approach and helps reinforce the value of lean thinking. And when undertaken with the staff or volunteers involved in the program or activity, it can be a valuable team-building exercise.

4. Analyze the results and start the evaluation process over again to make continuous improvements. A challenge for associations that involve volunteers in the process is that volunteers come and go and the approach must be continuous. It takes time, usually years, for organizations to fully embrace and incorporate lean thinking into the management of the enterprise. Just about the time volunteers "get it," they are likely to move on. Staff has to own lean thinking in an association, even if volunteers choose to get involved.

Living the Lean Process

In 2008, two associations in the Netherlands joined forces: the Central Trade Association for Home Furnishing Retailers and Mitex, which promotes the interests of Dutch fashion retailers. Known together now as CBW-MITEX, both had been challenged by declines in membership due to a tough economy. And both realized, based on a 2020 forecast that predicted a continually changing climate for retailers, that the challenge wasn't likely to disappear.

Three years after joining forces, the association completed a customer and employee satisfaction survey and hired a lean consultant to help improve processes. The effort required value stream mapping, an especially relevant exercise for the organization's contact center and its publication, *InDetail*. When process is captured step by step, it's often easy to see where waste occurs. The trick is to do something about it.

As a result of its efforts, CBW-MITEX gained a clearer picture regarding the amount and value of its member contacts, created standardization in registering member contact, optimized internal processes, and improved efficiency in planning member visits by business advisors. Further, it's reduced waste in the production of its journal. According to CBW-MITEX's CEO Jan Dirk van der Zee, "Our communication department mapped the value stream of the process to publish the magazine and we were shocked by its length—more than eight meters—and the number of wastes." (For the record, eight meters is more than 26 feet!) The organization also now realizes—and values—the amount of information available internally that was once overlooked. They now know that they were sitting on what they call a "mountain of pearls"—readily available data that enables them to work at a higher level of effectiveness. It took lean processes to help discover these pearls. Chances are you, too, have both the internal inefficiencies and the pearls!

Though the Association of American Medical Colleges started its process excellence approach in 2010 as a one-time strategic shift designed to help the association find the financial resources to launch new projects, the organization has since hired a full-time director of process excellence dedicated to leading these ongoing efforts. In one example, like CBX-Mitex, AAMC easily found ways to tighten its journal production process. Notes Mallon, "We had an inefficient process of getting publications out the door. Our new staff person has worked with our director of publishing, in-house designers, and publications staff to tighten work flows and expectations, including those for our authors and subject matter experts. Often, bottlenecks occurred with authors. Now, we are instituting metrics and measures to know whether or not we're hitting targets." Member management is another area in which expectations have been better defined and metrics have been put in place.

Realizing and embracing the concept of continuous improvement represents a new horizon for associations, as many are just now discovering. The benefits are many: reduced costs, increased effectiveness, accelerated turnaround time, decreased staff and member frustration, and perhaps most importantly, enhanced value. As the competitive environment heats up, who wouldn't want to score in any, or all, of these areas?

Role of the CEO

The board has to understand and support lean thinking. As we have said, agreeing on what has value will be difficult. Board members can have strong opinions, and staff can be reluctant to challenge these points of view, even when they are blatantly incorrect. The fact is that boards contribute significantly to association waste with well-intentioned but misguided ideas and direction, making it difficult to address the topic. This is why we suggested the improved composition of boards and the empowerment of the CEO in *Race for Relevance*. The right mix on the board makes it easier to discuss sensitive subjects. One CEO we know solved the problem by initiating a lean movement without informing the board. The result was fewer items in the catalog and increased profitability—and not one board member even noticed! Although we don't advocate acting outside the board, we understand that sometimes it's the only way to get things done. We do believe that boards should trust the staff to do their jobs and that boards should not be working in operational roles.

The CEO plays a critical role. He or she has to work with the leadership to gain support and defuse efforts that contradict a lean strategy. He or she sets the tone for staff, equips them with necessary tools, participates in the process, celebrates their successes, and sustains the momentum in changing the way staff thinks about value and processes. The CEO is a cheerleader, encouraging staff to reach the finish line when undertaking a program and service review.

One of the obstacles for the CEO and staff is workload. It's difficult to find the energy to tackle process improvements when one can barely complete each day's work. That's the irony: staff is often so busy working on projects that don't add value that they are unable to take on the challenge of closely reviewing current processes in an effort to increase efficiency and/or productivity. Associations are beginning to address this challenge by hiring consultants or staff with various types of process improvement skills and experience, in programs such as Lean, Six Sigma, CQI (Continuous Quality Improvement), or ISO 9000, to oversee initiatives. As noted previously, the American Association of Medical Colleges recently hired a full-time staff member to head its process improvement initiative. According to Bill Mallon, "Our director of process excellence, John Bubrick, is helping move away barriers that drive everyone crazy.... People are busy and don't necessarily have the skill set to figure out how to do things better. John comes in with this approach and the skills and tools that streamline workflow. Ultimately he is freeing people to do things they really want to do."

With the process improvement approach that the AAMC has adopted over the last two years—including retiring unnecessary software products, tightening staff travel policies, and shifting to enterprise technology solutions such as networked printers rather than individual printers— Mallon estimates that the association has had "hard cost" savings well over $250,000 per year, and that's just a start. "We are in the infancy of our process improvement focus—we have much more to do. But we are committed—our revised strategic priorities for the next two years include a goal to instill a culture of process excellence throughout the association."

Role of the Board

The board has to understand the underlying concepts of focusing on value and eliminating waste. This will be challenging in some associations but relatively easy in others. For example, a director on the board of a manufacturing trade association may understand it completely. Other directors may have been exposed to the concepts indirectly. An executive recently commented that his wife was a nurse and her hospital had recently undertaken lean approaches. One success for the hospital was reducing turnaround in the operating room from one hour to 20 minutes between operations.

At the start, the board has to be educated about the concept of continuous improvement. Using examples as close to their work or the field they operate in is the best strategy. Engaging them in a simplified exercise of value stream mapping could be illuminating. Have them map out the process for committees, from appointment, through meetings, to reporting or recommendation. Where are the bottlenecks that hold the process up? Where are committee members sitting idle, waiting for additional information or approvals? If a recommendation was not approved, what led to the failure of capitalizing on the committee members' time?

Don't forget, new board members should be briefed about lean concepts and processes during their orientation. (You do have an orientation and training, don't you?) Be as specific as possible regarding your efforts to ensure both understanding and future support.

Value Steam Resources

Appendix A has resources that will be helpful in your value stream mapping and continuous improvement efforts.

We also recommend that you conduct a search for lean process articles or publications in your specific profession, industry, or trade. There is a good chance that someone in your field is applying the concepts. The closer to home you can find applications, the better.

To be competitive, an association must be lean, maximizing productivity by focusing on significance and eliminating activity and effort that don't contribute to value. Inefficiency affects the association's competitiveness by wasting valuable resources. Lean thinking can involve a difficult transition from "that's the way we've always done it" attitudes. Associations must raise the bar when it comes to appraising the value of their programs and activities, systematically analyze their processes and value streams, continuously look for opportunities for improvement and waste reduction, and define waste as anything that does not contribute to member value or increase operational efficiency. Finally, thinking lean can help associations find the resources to enhance value, create new programs or services, or provide a boost to activities that are under-resourced. For association staff and volunteers alike, these benefits are incentive to undertake lean processes as a means of operating in the new normal.

Living Lean

ASSOCIATION: American Speech-Language-Hearing Association (ASHA)

BUDGET: $50 million

NUMBER OF STAFF MEMBERS: 260

NUMBER OF MEMBERS: 150,241

Members and affiliates of the American Speech-Language-Hearing Association (ASHA) annually pay membership dues and certification fees and often need proof of current certification status to be hired. Because the ASHA identification card is the gold standard many employers require, members asked if they could receive their cards more quickly after paying renewal dues and fees.

The solution? Living lean. The process began with a three-day facilitated meeting. The objectives:

- To train members of the dues-invoicing team on basic lean principles;
- To improve communication and understanding among departments;
- To create solutions to problems with the dues renewal process; and
- To create an action plan to implement changes to better serve members by providing faster turnaround from payment to card issuance.

The association created a "current state map" (also known as value stream mapping) listing every task in the process. Process and wait times were assigned for each task. The map graphically illustrated the problems in the process. Because of the obstacles, some members waited more than a month to receive their identification card. This occurred because of:

- Category changes for membership type;
- An outdated card format that was causing unnecessary lag time at the outsourced printer;
- Payment processing by third-party payers; and
- Inadequate staff resources for processing payments.

Once the problems were identified, the association focused on creating a list of root causes, which was particularly helpful when used with question starters to help participants sharpen their awareness of the problems. Starters included:

- How might...?
- How to...?
- In what ways might...?
- What might be all the...?

During this questioning exercise, staffers realized that clarifying the renewal process for members would solve a number of problems. They also discovered that redesigning the identification card so it could be produced in high-volume printers would alleviate lag time. (Notice how a complex problem can often be addressed with a simple solution. That's part of the process of lean operations.)

With the problems and potential solutions identified, the staff created an action plan for implementation, including the following:

- Encouraging members to renew online by communicating that it is the fastest way for them to receive their identification cards;
- Changing renewal FAQs to clearly state the procedures for third-party payments;
- Developing a general and detailed list of instructions for steps used to process bank lockbox payments;
- Designing a new member identification card that could be produced in high-volume printers; and
- Printing and mailing member cards twice a week.

As a result of lean processing, the association brought card production and mailing in house. Cards are now mailed within a day or two of receiving payments. Online renewals are up 50 percent over 2008, the year lean processes began. Now more than 100,000 ASHA members renew online each year—roughly two thirds of the membership. There have been cost savings as well. The association previously spent $26,000 per year for a vendor to ship cards. They've since purchased the folder/insert machine necessary for the job for $25,000. The cost savings over three years has been significant. Other departments are using the machine as well, saving additional dollars, and ASHA is seeing what many associations discover: Increased savings and efficiencies in one area often spilled over into others.

CHAPTER TEN

Purposeful Abandonment

"The art of leadership is saying no,
not yes. It is very easy to say yes."
— Tony Blair[69]

We have saved the toughest strategic concept for last: purposeful abandonment. It's tough because it goes against the natural flow of increasing member value by adding, not subtracting, programs and services.

As we have pointed out, association efforts that don't build on strength are unlikely to perform in a competitive landscape. The imperative of concentrating on core programs and services means the marginal ones have to go. The need for fit means the misfits have to go. The activities and benefits that don't add meaningful value are wasteful, and they have to go.

As we have noted in earlier chapters, everybody wants to add a new service, introduce a new program, or launch a new benefit. But rarely is a board, committee, individual, or group interested in eliminating services or activities. Everybody wants to add. Nobody wants to subtract. Nobody, to our knowledge, ever pursued a position on an association board with the intent of eliminating programs and services. Few, if any, CEOs take an association job with the promise to eliminate programs and services.

Elimination is counterintuitive and, thus, hard to do. But that's why it's powerful.

In the retail world, there is an inventory situation called "over assorted." In this condition a store is trying to offer too much. It has every type, size, model, color, and version imaginable. The result is mass confusion. The customer is overwhelmed. Finding things is difficult and frustrating. (Think about the last time you were in the drug store trying to find a specific cold medicine or in the cereal aisle in a supermarket trying to find your kids' favorite brand.) And it is likely that products in demand will be out of stock, while inventory is invested in unwanted goods.

Retailers have recognized the considerable downsides of trying to offer too much and have undertaken SKU reduction initiatives. (A SKU is a "stock keeping unit," a unique item or product. Today's supermarkets can have more than 20,000 SKUs.) Every year hundreds of new products or "new and improved" items are launched. Retailers understand that they have to rigorously purge marginal products or their inventories will spin out of control, resulting in bewildered customers who simply walk away.

The tendency of associations is to continue to add programs and services without the critical process to discontinue those that have lost their appeal, those that never lived up to expectations, those that continue to require bigger and bigger subsidies, and those that are uncompetitive.

All the Reasons for Keeping Everything

Understanding why volunteers and staff are reluctant to discontinue programs or activities is helpful. Here is what we hear:

- The service is used by a few members. It is providing them with something of value and a reason for them to renew. Why not keep it?

- The program doesn't take much to offer. What's the harm in keeping it? (You saw what it takes in our example in Chapter 4.)

- We made a considerable financial investment in developing and launching this service. Are we going to eliminate something that cost us so much?

- After all the hoopla we made about this new venture, won't we have egg on our face if we abandon it? Won't this be perceived as a major failure?

- Volunteers made major commitments of time to make this new service a reality. How can we tell them that their efforts were wasted?

- If we eliminate programs and services, won't it look like we are doing less for our members? Won't it look like less for the same dues?

Abandonment: The Key to Innovation

Believe it or not, abandonment plays a critical role in innovation. As noted earlier, there is a big difference between generating ideas/being creative and true innovation. No innovation takes place until there is a service, activity, or product in the market that is accepted and valued. Developing a valued member service and gaining its adoption in the market is a considerable undertaking, one that requires time, expertise, financial investment, and marketing support—an undertaking that requires resources not just to produce but to maintain.

With increasing member scrutiny of dues and the unprecedented levels of competition in the marketplace, few associations have resources lying around idle waiting to support a new initiative. An early question in the innovation process is, "Where are we going to get the resources to make this happen?" In most cases, the resources are sitting right under your nose. That's the good news. The bad news is that while the resources are readily available, they are currently allocated to other services or activities. You will have to take the resources needed to innovate away from existing programs.

Abandonment is not just about getting rid of obsolete activities. It has an even more important role: providing critical resources for innovation and tomorrow's relevance. It is about taking resources allocated to yesterday's activities and redirecting them to the services that will add value tomorrow.

Abandonment: The Key to the Technology Challenge

One challenge most associations share is in the complex, fast-moving, and difficult-to-navigate technology arena. We are convinced that much of the road to relevance is on what was formerly referred to as the "information highway." Unfortunately, traffic moves fast on highways, and associations are traditionally slow and deliberate in making decisions and taking action. But probably the biggest challenge confronting associations in technology is the resources problem. Where are we going to find the money to maintain and upgrade our systems? Where are we going to find the time and energy to explore and exploit new technologies? Where is the staff to develop and support our technology initiatives going to come from?

With most associations dealing with resource restraints, scrutiny of dues, and increasing overhead, the funding for technology is not likely to be lying around idle. As noted earlier, we believe the technology spend for associations—the percentage of annual revenue allocated to the people and systems for the organization's technology—will have to increase substantially in the coming years from the current average of around 4 percent to perhaps three times that in the near future.

Where is the money going to come from? You will have to take it away from other delivery systems, activities, and programs. But to do that, you will have to develop a compelling case for what the technology is going to look like and what it will deliver.

Imagine an association with a state-of-the-art website that is not in constant need of upgrade, that members can navigate intuitively, that delivers answers and solutions effortlessly, and that is integrated with the association's database, webinars, and social media sites. That would be powerful, wouldn't it?

Imagine an association with a real social media presence, not a superficial "We're on Facebook" effort, but an association that has someone on staff or on contract to focus solely on posting information, stimulating dialogue, and researching content. This would be an association that meaningfully integrates social media with its conferences and events.

Imagine an association with a database or customer relationship management (CRM) system that tracks member behavior, knows member preferences, measures member engagement, effortlessly targets member communication and information, and has staff or part-time independent contractors constantly updating member data and harvesting new prospect information.

Imagine an association with the capabilities to go beyond adopting technologies to exploring emerging technologies, with sufficient staff to actually flirt with the cutting edge, with staff or an independent contractor who has time to test new applications and try emerging technologies in their very early stages. In retrospect, what if an association had the vision and wherewithal to assign a full-time staff member with sole responsibility for social media in 2004, the year Facebook was launched? Think of where that association would be now!

Develop a picture of the future technology platform for your association. Outline what it will take in financial and staff resources. Then propose abandoning the programs, services, or initiatives that don't add comparable value, that aren't viable in tomorrow's environment, or that don't fit with the association's core strengths. This "purposeful abandonment"—not abandonment for abandonment's sake—will greatly increase your odds of success in getting the resources you need in the technology arena that is critical to your relevance.

What Associations Can Learn from Steve Jobs

One high-profile executive who understood the power of abandonment was Steve Jobs. Throughout his career his mantra was "focus." In the late 70s, along with Steve Wozniak and Mike Markkula, he developed a simple, "Apple Marketing Philosophy." According to Walter Isaacson, Jobs' official biographer, the philosophy's second point was: "To be successful, Apple should center its efforts on accomplishing its main goals and eliminate all the 'unimportant opportunities.'"[70]

During Jobs' twelve year absence (1985–1997), Apple went through a period of product proliferation. The company got into the printer business and server business, and its product line expanded significantly with dozens of versions of items like the Macintosh.

When Jobs returned, he conducted a comprehensive product line review. He quickly directed the elimination of 70 percent of the Apple product line, according to one account. He decided that Apple would focus on just four products: a professional desktop, professional portable computer, a consumer desktop (that became the iMac), and a consumer portable.[71]

The massive abandonment of a bloated product line and the clear focus on just four products saved Apple from potential bankruptcy. It may seem inconceivable today, but in 1997, many thought that that Apple was not going to survive. Jobs' strategy not only saved Apple, it fueled a turn-around from a $1.04 billion loss in 1997 to a $309 million profit in 1998, not bad numbers from a "shrink-to-grow" strategy!

An interesting side note of particular interest to association executives is that Apple's board did not support Job's drastic strategy. According to Issacson, "At first the board pushed back. It was a risk, Jobs was told. 'I can make it work,' he replied. The board never voted on the new strategy. Jobs was in charge, and he forged ahead."[72] Sometimes that's what an empowered association CEO needs to do as well. (However, we certainly recommend the endorsement of the board!) There is a lesson here for association executives and boards alike. Apple had a board populated with high-powered executives and they did not see the power of focus and the need to prune an overgrown product line. A board that included the CEOs or former CEOs of Oracle, IBM, Intuit, Chrysler, and DuPont did not understand the debilitating consequences of an overextended, compli-cated, and confusing product line.

Think about it. If a board composed of these captains of industry didn't get it, how likely is it that your average association board, made up of volunteers (no offense to volunteers), will? Many, especially in profes-sional societies, will admit that their board members come up short when it comes to business acumen. The bottom line: The association's CEO must be the advocate for abandonment. The CEO is in the best position to see abandonment's potential. The board is likely more comfortable with the status quo and the false safety net of offering a large number of benefits, even if performance is lagging. The CEO is best prepared to understand and manage the associated risks; the board will prefer to play it safe and stick with the status quo. The CEO has to take charge and forge ahead. A smart board will understand and be supportive.

How to Abandon

As we have said, jettisoning a program, service, or activity is a challenge, almost always a daunting, seemingly insurmountable challenge. It can appear that the deck is stacked against you. So how do you go about abandoning yesterday so you can realize tomorrow?

Don't underestimate the challenge.

If, as a CEO, you think this will be easy, think again. Anticipate pushback. Start with the six common responses to the suggestion to eliminate we listed earlier in this chapter. Add a few of your own based on what you know about your board or influential members. Know that you will have to put together a strong, defensible case. Initially, opposition is almost guaranteed to outweigh support.

Don't go it alone.

Recruiting a team to help advance your recommendations is essential. Make sure this team has the savvy to navigate the association's political waters. At the minimum, include senior staff and the executive committee. Provide them with the data and talking points they need to convince others. If your executive committee doesn't buy in, you may choose to wait until they do. Or you may choose to keep them informed regarding your progress but move ahead without their blessing, understanding that ensuring efficient operations and maximizing the association's resources is one of your responsibilities as CEO.

Identify a compelling opportunity and then propose abandonment.

Start by identifying a major opportunity for the association: a new or considerably enhanced service, an initiative with significant potential, something that everyone will immediately agree will take the association in the right direction or will make a big difference for members. Once you have this undertaking or value-added opportunity well defined, then identify the resources that will be required to realize it.

Once you've completed the above three steps (and only then), you are ready to ask the board or staff to let go of existing programs or activities that don't compare to the promise of the new enterprise. It's like when a toddler gets hold of a sharp or dangerous object. If you ask him to give it to you, what will he say? "No!" But if you take a shiny, new, fun item in your hand, shake it in front of him, and ask if he'd like it, he'll drop the dangerous object for the splashier new one. We're not suggesting boards are like toddlers. But we are suggesting that it's easier to let something go when there is the promise of something better on the horizon.

We recently worked with a professional society with a very weak annual conference. It was a distant third or fourth among competitive meetings. It lost money. Numerous attempts to find the right formula to give it meaning and position had failed. But there was a strong, 25-year tradition behind it and there was no will to pull the plug. That was until a strategic planning session identified two opportunities: a major advancement in the society's technology platform and the potential to revitalize the chapter structure with a redesigned model. Both initiatives required resources that were not available. All eyes turned to the conference and the considerable time and expense that it consumed. The vote was unanimous. Discontinue the conference. Shift the resources to technology and the chapter redesign. Without the promise of new technology and chapter revitalization, the lame conference—a poor use of considerable resources—would still be around.

Use data.

Nothing works like the facts, particularly when people have an emotional attachment to something you want them to give up. And you will have to deal with emotional investments in services that didn't measure up to expectations, cultural ties to programs the association has supported since its inception ("What will the founders say?"), and traditions that defy rational analysis. Use the following data points when developing your case:

Costs. Far too frequently associations don't know what it costs to support a service or what it takes to sustain an activity. (Don't feel bad; most businesses are notorious for not knowing their true costs either.) Most know the direct costs (Meetings, for example, include the cost of hotel rooms, meeting space, meals, refreshment breaks, etc.) but fail to allocate staff and overhead costs. This limited calculation creates a false sense of generating a profit. In other situations, it understates the real level of resources required. Make sure all the costs associated with a program or activity are identified. Sometimes, you can make a convincing case just by conducting an accurate accounting of the resources really required for a program. The costs of some activities, like a House of Delegates meeting or a legislative event, can produce jaw-dropping responses when all the direct, staff, and overhead costs are finally accounted for.

When confronted with a $150,000 bill for a meeting that produces little value (or worse, a boondoggle with no real value), staff and leaders must answer the tough question: "Knowing the true cost of this event, is it really the best use of our limited resources?"

We recently came across a large professional society that did a comprehensive analysis of all the costs associated with convening their Congress of Delegates. The amount of staff time was astounding. No one had ever given it much thought. Hundreds upon hundreds of hours were required to develop reports, write motions, and provide liaisons to committees in preparation for the congress. The total bill: $1.1 million! The contribution the congress made to the organization and the profession was modest at best and certainly not worth the bill once it was tallied up.

Another organization began to count the "absence cost" of its House of Delegates, all of whom were self-employed. Absence cost refers to revenue forgone by members while they conduct the business of the association. Though it is not an actual expenditure, it can be an instructive figure. To determine it for your members (whether self-employed or not), estimate the average earned income per member hour and multiply it by the average number of hours spent in the session (or at board meetings) each year. (Factor in travel time, too, if you like.) Then multiply by the number of delegates (or board members). This is the opportunity cost of your governance. Again, the number can be staggering—and a motivation for change.

Participation. Data on member participation in or use of programs and services varies from association to association. Simply compiling trend information on attendance at educational seminars, participation in insurance programs, or use of discount offerings can be illuminating. A quick calculation can show the percentage of members who are either validating or challenging the value of the service or the relevance of the activity. Board and staff should agree on a threshold level of use required to maintain a service or activity. Exceptions can be considered, but shouldn't a program or service be capable of attracting five percent of the membership? Ten percent of the membership? If a service is so valuable and an activity is so important, shouldn't it be capable of attracting even a modest share of the membership?

How meaningful is an association offering that only a fraction of the membership uses? Caution: Despite the admonition to use data, be careful when comparing your group to others. It may not be unusual for a small, niche association to attract 30 percent of members to an annual meeting but unrealistic for a large, international association to do the same. More valuable information may be historical data for your group. Watch for downward trends, as they can be illuminating. Further, when evaluating your activities, consider not only the numbers but also the objectives. If they are being met, the participation number may not be as important.

Competition. Just saying that "there's a lot of competition out there" is inadequate. Use the competitive analysis matrix offered earlier in this book to help you get a handle on what you are up against. List all the providers of continuing education and their courses for a year. List all the insurance brokers and agents that sell into your market. List all the publications, newsletters, and blogs that target your member market. And don't forget all the consultants' and vendors' content marketing efforts; this is a growing source of competition in almost all professions and industries.

Pose questions about the competition: Since members have ample access to this service, why are we offering it? What makes our program or service unique? Are we a "me, too" with little real value? What would happen if we discontinued or sold this service (assuming someone would actually buy it!)?

Agree that something big must go.

Don't get trapped in "nibbling around the edges." Eliminating minor marginal activities is important. They collectively eat up a lot more resources than most people realize. But the big dividends are going to come when the association has the courage to let a significant program or service area go. This is when real resources are unleashed for redirection to opportunity and innovation.

Most associations have what they consider to be a major area of service or activity that they could totally walk away from and be better off for it. Many don't have permission to seriously consider doing so, however. One approach is to set a goal in the abandonment process. From the start, agree that something big is going on the chopping block, something that will free up a staff person from a major responsibility or something that will free up a significant budget allocation (10 to 20 percent of the budget). This will set the bar at a level that will make you think big and avoid chipping away at the edges. To perform in the new normal, you have to "go big or go home."

For example, a state trade association was struggling with its ability to execute across multiple product and service lines. And it recognized significant opportunities to increase government advocacy because legislation and regulatory activity were sharply on the rise. From the outside, it was apparent that if they would abandon their entire educational program, considerable resources would be freed up without a risk to membership. The educational offerings were being used by less than 15 percent of the membership. They lost money, requiring subsidy from dues income. The national association offered conferences and webinars that duplicated what the state association was offering, and courses similar to those of the state organization were available from local associations.

In this case, one and a half staff positions out of eight could be reallocated. Direct costs for seminars and conferences could be eliminated. But the association never gathered the data or put a case together. Tradition easily won over strategic thinking. "Education is something an association is supposed to do. The members expect it." (And equally important, no one made a compelling "opportunity case.") The legislation and regulation of their industry was increasing dramatically, resulting in market limitations and increased cost of compliance for member companies. The association had the resources—allocated to unnecessary educational programs—to add one and a half lobbyists, which would have more than doubled its government affairs staffing. But it's hard to make changes when traditions and loss of some staff in favor of others are on the line.

Contrast this with the Greater New York Chapter of the Association of Fundraising Professionals (AFP). The chapter, with fewer than 1,000 members, was in a state of decline when the Kellen Company took the helm, and took a close look at operations. None of the group's signature events—Fundraising Day in New York (FRDNY), the Chamberlain Luncheon, and National Philanthropy Day (NPD) Luncheon—were close to netting budgeted revenue and one was losing money, yet all required tremendous effort to produce.

The Chamberlain Luncheon was the venue for the chapter's award luncheon. Though the award had merit, the luncheon lost money. Rather than abandoning the concept outright, the association cleverly moved the award presentation to National Philanthropy Day, another of its signature events. (Abandonment by combination can be less painful and just as effective.) Moving the award brought a new audience to National Philanthropy Day, so income covered the event's budget and more.

Further, Fundraising Day in New York, an event for 1,500-plus attendees, has been in the same venue for years. It's an intricate educational program with simultaneous tracks. Before the down economy, FRDNY was known to bring in revenue for the chapter, covering operational costs and adding to its reserves. The new normal changed the game, and the association needed to increase revenue and decrease expenses. The following changes made a difference and saved both the event and the chapter's overall budget:

- For the first time, audiovisual was put out for bid. This saved approximately $5,000. (As it turned out, in a last-minute twist, the hotel matched the price to keep the business in house.)

- A VIP reception before lunch was cut. No one missed it and the chapter saved $1,500.

- The association encouraged vendors to pay by check for a discount, rather than by credit card (saving bank fees).

- A planning committee breakfast at the venue, which previously cost $2,000, was renegotiated as a complimentary service provided by the venue.

- An in-kind program with benefits and new annual sponsorship offerings cut out expenses for items such as tote bags, photography, and advertising.

In AFP's case, abandonment didn't mean total elimination—but it did mean leaving behind the way "they had always done it." And though a new management company provided both an excuse and an incentive to review the chapter's signature events, your association doesn't have to wait for a fresh set of eyes. And trust us, it's better to let something go because you choose to, rather than because you have to. "Have to" is much more painful. We've seen and heard that over and over again from the associations we work with.

Ask good questions.

Abandonment is an excellent opportunity to practice the art of asking good questions. Absent a financial catastrophe, the cultural subtext, emotional factors, and strong traditions in associations make the right approach critical. A confrontational approach is likely to generate pushback and entrench people in their positions. Asking strategic questions is a more effective tactic. The following table illustrates alternatives:

Statement	Question
This program is losing money.	Shouldn't we expect this program to perform better financially? What is a reasonable expectation of net revenue from this program?
Members hated this program.	Evaluations weren't stellar. How can we rework this program?
Nobody is attending this event.	What is the trend information on attendance at this event?
The competition is killing us on this service.	What is the extent of competition for this service? How are we positioned vis-à-vis the competition?
Only older members attend this event.	What's necessary to draw a more diverse age demo-graphic to this event? Are there things we can do to re-energize and refresh it?
We don't have any business offering this product.	How is this product related to our mission?

Capitalize on difficult times or poor financial performance.

This sounds harsh, but an association board is more receptive to change when the association is feeling pain. The Great Recession of 2008 was an excellent opportunity to challenge marginal services and activities. The boards we worked with were more open to new ideas than ever before. Challenging economic conditions, decreased memberships, and declining attendance at meetings stressed even the most financially strong associations during the recession and continue to challenge many today because of the new normal. Crisis often provides an excellent window of opportunity to clean house.

In good times, marginal programs aren't noticed. In bad times, marginal programs are magnified. It becomes easier to say, "You know, when times were good, we could subsidize this program. But now that we have pressure on every expense line, we are cutting staff, and we just cannot afford the luxury of sustaining this program. The cost is simply not justified given the economy and our financial situation."

It doesn't take a full recession. Any time you are confronted with a financial challenge, a revenue shortfall, or an unanticipated expense, use the opportunity to challenge programs that are obsolete, underperforming, or losing luster. Making this a habit benefits the association in the long run and prevents volunteer decision makers from becoming complacent.

Adopt a "one in, one out" policy.

First, agree that the association has a full plate and that staff is already stretched too thin. Then get agreement that if anybody proposes a new program or activity, an existing service has to go to make room for it. Like "revenue neutral" practices, associations need "activity neutral" policies to keep their plates from overflowing. Refer to the supermarket analogy. Stores have only so much shelf space, so when a new product or an improved version is introduced, something has to go to make room. What association service or program is going to be dropped so there is space for the new?

Set review dates when programs are added.

The plethora of association programs and activities exists because associations don't regularly review performance. From today on, make it policy that any new program or service adopted must be reviewed within a specific time. It may be six months, a year, or three years. Make sure a deadline is part of the proposal. For increased effectiveness, consider identifying how performance will be measured. Break-even status? Profitability? Member usage? Member satisfaction surveys? Knowing your performance standards upfront will encourage you to collect the data you need for a fair review when the time comes.

Take your time.

Members are suspicious when you try to rush an initiative even if you're doing it because you are in dire straits. Take the time to explain what you are doing and why. Let volunteer leaders (and members at large when appropriate) have time to think about what you are proposing. The bigger the initiative, the more time it takes. We've seen many proposals that were unsuccessful simply because they were rushed.

Abandon in Order to Add

Abandonment is an essential strategy for well-being. Though difficult, it pays. It is an important complement to the first four strategies in the book: build on strength, concentrate resources, integrate programs and services for good fit, and adopt lean thinking to use people and processes effectively.

Consider this: Is Ford in better shape than it was in 2009? Is General Motors in better shape than it was in 2009? Of course, they are. Why? Because both of these companies recognized the power of focus and the need to abandon to survive in a highly competitive market in tough economic conditions.

Ford abandoned Volvo, Jaguar, Land Rover, and Aston Martin to concentrate on just two brands: Ford and Lincoln. GM abandoned Saab, Oldsmobile, Pontiac, and Hummer to focus primarily on just two brands: Chevrolet and Cadillac. (They also kept Buick because it is wildly popular in China.)

Ford and General Motors recognized that the broad product lines that served them well in the past were flawed for today and the future. Both had to go through gut-wrenching decisions to jettison major brands that they had invested billions in over the years. Was it easy? Absolutely not. Did it work? Unquestionably. Associations will benefit by doing the same thing.

Role of the CEO

Helping the association abandon programs and services that are losing money, have low market share, or never lived up to expectations may be one of the CEO's toughest jobs. Doing so requires assessing performance and may appear to be passing judgment on past activities or indicting the work of past volunteers. Using data to build a case will professionalize the process and make it easier for boards to abandon activities that they themselves may have been involved in bringing to life.

It's helpful to develop a system for periodic product and service review. This is an area in which the CEO can be helpful. Further, he or she can work with staff to develop a protocol to measure potential new products before they are even considered. The tougher the approval process on the front end, the less likely the need for abandonment on the back end. Finally, the CEO can hold the board to the "one in, one out" policy, making recommendations about what should be considered for abandonment when new offerings are considered.

The Role of the Board

As with all the strategies, it is up to the board to fully partner with the CEO. Doing so may be uncomfortable when it comes to abandoning products and services. It will likely take courage, as some board members may be unhappy with the concept. We've worked with many leaders who don't see the value of a narrow product and service offering for the reasons outlined earlier. And it's tough to face a colleague when you've voted against retaining a service they are passionate about or a product they helped introduce.

Board members must also address fear: the fear of making a wrong decision, of upsetting colleagues, of reducing relevance by getting rid of services (even if they are only used by a small portion of the membership), and of facing the political ramifications to their future aspirations within the association if they make unpopular decisions. Asking board members to sign a document detailing their responsibilities to the association is one way to address these fears. Board members who are clear regarding their roles and responsibilities often have a greater sense of clarity regarding decisions when it comes to strategy.

Finally, the board can play an important role in articulating and supporting how resources from an abandoned program or activity can provide the fuel needed for the new service or the critical technology initiatives on the association's road to relevance.

Case Study

Purposeful Abandonment Leads to Purposeful Pricing

ASSOCIATION: Associated General Contractors of St. Louis

BUDGET: $3,300,000

NUMBER OF STAFF MEMBERS: 18

NUMBER OF MEMBERS: 425 firms

The economic downturn of 2008 took a toll on the construction industry and simultaneously provided an opportunity for Associated General Contractors of St. Louis to take a close look at all it was doing on behalf of members.

Led by Len Toenjes, CAE, president, the association embarked on a methodical and thorough examination of its programs and services. Key staff created a list of 140 items. Says Toenjes, "I don't think anybody on our staff really had a good, clear picture of just how many different things we were doing. I don't think we understood the breadth of it all until we really sat down and captured it."

The inventory was eclectic. Anything that used any of the association's resources or time (staff or volunteer) showed up, including the board and executive committee, publications, social events, and training programs. "It was a real learning experience for our staff to be able to get a clear vision of where all their time went. The things they assumed were just happening weren't just happening."

Once the list was complete, Toenjes and his team spent time force-ranking items according to a variety of categories. (For more on the process, see *Race for Relevance: 5 Radical Changes for Associations,* pages 112–114. We've also included the matrix in Appendix B of this publication for your convenience.) Though they had planned to ask the board to do the same ranking, the task was too large to duplicate with the board and they settled for reporting results to the board. "It was eye-opening to them also," notes Toenjes.

Though there were many benefits for the association, the main one is that the association is now focused on what's most important. "We eliminated more than 30 programs. We made a significant cut. That's helped us focus better." In addition, the board requested a review of current financial performance for each item. The final report created by the staff and approved by the board categorized each program, project, or service as one to continue as is, make modifications to improve performance, or discontinue.

The financial aspect of this process was also eye-opening. Toenjes says, "During the initial evaluation, every one of my vice presidents called and asked to speak to me privately. Each said, 'We're losing money on my programs and I feel really bad about it.' I knew once they got the picture of what was happening it would help them focus on the reality of their pricing." In this case, purposeful abandonment also led to purposeful pricing.

One not-so-surprising note: Uncomfortable with the idea of completely abandoning some beloved programs, the board asked Toenjes to move them to a "holding tank" instead of putting them on the cutting block. Items in the tank include inactive committees, printed publications, and nonperforming affinity programs. It's interesting to note the commonalities in these programs and services: They all seemed like good ideas at the time of inception, yet over time their lack of use proved they were either initially misguided or totally outdated.

An unexpected aspect of the abandonment process was educational. Staff members didn't fully understand what each other did; and as the team worked together on ranking programs and services, they learned new things about various aspects of the association's operations. In some cases, the board had to be educated as well. Toenjes calls this unexpected benefit a "tremendous educational component."

Another unexpected benefit was the discussion across departments. Though intensely time consuming (some rankings took as long as an hour or two per evaluation) the process resulted in team building, as staff members learned new things and understood each other's work better.

Toenjes admits he had to be a cheerleader and work with the staff team to remain dedicated to the process. The effort paid off, he says. "There's no doubt that we're operating more efficiently. There's no doubt that we've been able to reduce expenses. We're better able to make an allocation of where our dues are going. It's helped us reprice a number of things we were doing. And it's really brought our staff together to help them understand their interrelatedness as far as where dollars go and as far as how their pricing affects the whole operation."

CHAPTER ELEVEN

CEO and Board Roles (and Potholes) on the Road

"Wherever I've seen a nonprofit institution with a strong board that gives the right kind of leadership, it represented very hard work on the part of the chief executive officer— not only to bring the right people on the board but to meld them into a team and point them in the right direction."

– PETER DRUCKER[73]

As we have noted in each chapter, there are roles for the association's CEO and roles for the board on the road to relevance. Optimum performance will come only when both parties understand the parts they play and complement and support one another. Valuable human capital will be wasted if roles aren't clear. Disputing who does what, crossing the line into each other's turf, and questioning who is responsible for what causes delays and waste. And all this wasted human capital is the most valuable of the association's resources: the board and CEO.

Let's start with simple role delineations. In *Boards that Make a Difference: A New Design for Leadership in Nonprofit and Public Organizations*,[74] John Carver uses the "ends" and "means" definitions. The board decides what is to be accomplished, the "ends" or outcomes. The CEO is responsible for how those ends are to be achieved, the "means."

The CEO is the association's steward of strategy. A steward is "a person who manages another's property or financial affairs; one who administers anything as the agent of another or others." The CEO manages the association's strategy. The board directs and controls strategy. First, they (with the CEO's input) define the priorities and direction for the association. (One of their most important roles is to make the concentration decision.) Then the board has to hold the CEO and themselves accountable for performance and ensure that the priorities are, in fact achieved and the association is on course.

The effective board understands the importance of empowering the CEO with the stewardship of the association's strategy. There are three basic reasons the CEO should be the strategy steward:

- **Continuity.** Continuity of purpose is a critical element of success. The association can't be constantly changing its answer to the concentration decision. The association has to continuously eliminate waste and improve productivity. The association has to purposely and regularly abandon the old to make resources available for the new. These efforts aren't one-time deals. They are ongoing. The CEO has continuity, boards don't. In fact, if you think about it, boards are discontinuous by design, with director turnover built in.

- **Resource knowledge.** Skillful, creative, and disciplined use of resources implies that whoever is managing them knows what they are and how they are deployed. Even the most diligent board member, time-pressed with a full-time job, is unlikely to gain a comprehensive, meaningful grasp of the association's resources, particularly in a large association. The CEO is far more informed regarding where resources are being deployed and how they might be used best.

- **Consequence awareness.** A CEO is on the job every day and sees how resource allocations are working and where they are not being optimized. The CEO will immediately feel the consequences of misappropriated resources or see where needed resources are lacking. Ongoing adjustments are required. A board meeting several times a year just isn't enough to create the feel of the road.

The candid board will agree that there are three additional factors that limit the board's capacity in overseeing the association's strategy:

- **Political interference.** Let's face it: Internal politics can make difficult and disciplined decision making challenging. Sometimes it is easier and more comfortable for the typical board to make politically based decisions rather than resource-based decisions, especially if the decision has far-reaching and unpopular ramifications. (This is why many associations are still stuck with chapters despite declining participation, lack of volunteers to run them, and duplication of services within the organizational structure.)

- **Time pressures.** This is not easy work. Implementing the five strategic concepts will take considerable time and effort. It won't likely happen if left to time-pressed officers and directors.

- **Board composition.** As we've noted repeatedly, few boards are composed for performance. As a result, they bring a wide range of characteristics and talents to the table, some more beneficial than others. Having the knowledge, motivation, and discipline to implement strategic concepts may or may not be among them.

Bottom line: The board and CEO must work together as partners for the association to thrive. There must be candor. There must be respect. And the environment must be safe enough for disagreement when necessary. The larger the board, the harder it is to achieve the comfort it takes to create this environment. Even when it is achieved, however, governance is not easy. Consider the following detours on the road to relevance:

"We're Member-Driven"

We've heard the "member driven" versus "staff driven" conversations for years. Really, who cares who is driving the bus if the association is effective, offers high member value, and is helping members work less stressfully, more profitably, and more productively? Yet we've seen boards worry and wring their hands and heard past presidents say, "This is a member-driven association, and the board should be directing the association's resources. This approach is giving too much authority to the staff."

By setting priorities and offering direction that guides resource allocation, the board is directing the association's resources. Realistically, most
board members don't give much thought to association business until
they are preparing for a board meeting. In the meantime, staff is handling
the day-to-day worries and operations. That's what they are being paid for.

Instead of worrying about who's driving the association, why not adopt
a blended term: "member directed, staff driven"? Rather than an either/
or, we like this "both" terminology. It suggests a partnership. It promotes
teamwork. And it acknowledges that both groups (board members and
staff) have specific roles to play in association operations.

Next time someone uses "member driven," ask them exactly what they
mean. It could lead to an interesting and valuable discussion.

The Renegade Director

How do you deal with the director who continues to cross the line,
delving into the details of execution and specific resource allocations?
Members of the board must understand the importance of challenging
their peers. This is not easy. Feelings can get hurt. Relationships can get
frayed. How the behavior is addressed is critical. The use of questions
can be very helpful. "Do you think that the CEO and staff can handle
this?" "Do you really think that this is something that the board needs to
address?" "Is there a reason that the board needs to delve so deeply into
this?" Keep in mind one of our favorite guidelines: If somebody else can
do it, it is not the work of the board.

The Political Impasse

Let's say you're on the road to relevance. You are using lean approaches
and mapping processes to identify waste and make improvements. What
happens when an objective assessment of board and committee processes
results in proposals for change that aren't popular, such as staffing
changes that will affect a much-loved senior staff member or suggestions
to change the roles of long-serving volunteers?

This is another political situation that can be challenging. In one
situation, an association had a leadership development committee that
identified and recruited directors for the board. It also had a nominating committee consisting of the five most recent past presidents

that nominated the chairman-elect. A review of the processes for both committees identified redundancies in committee functioning, staffing consequences, and travel expenses that could be eliminated if the committees were combined. But who wants to tell the past presidents? We've seen many cases where it's deemed easier (and safer) to do nothing rather than pursue changes that would position the association for a stronger, more relevant future. A better response would be to call in some enlightened past presidents to help with the discussion.

Avoiding Potholes in the Road to Relevance

The road to relevance is long. Adopting new ways of governing and managing is challenging. Pushback and resistance often keep raising their ugly heads. How do the board and CEO maintain the stamina to respond to the ongoing challenge?

Even when changes have been agreed upon and are being implemented, it is easy to slip back into the old way of doing things. People will be inclined to want to go back to structures and processes that they are comfortable with, regardless of their ineffectiveness. It can be draining for staff and volunteers alike to stay on course. Further, the old guard is going to be around for a while and may look for the change makers to stumble so they can advocate a return to the traditions of the past.

A courageous, knowledgeable board is necessary on the road to relevance. Everything we've written about in this book is easier with enlightened volunteers. Keep this in mind as you are recruiting future leaders. Know that they must be oriented. Provide them with the background and information they need to understand your strategic goals. Take time to answer their questions and ensure understanding. And recognize that board turnover makes this an ongoing process.

10 Things the Board Should Do to Support Association Strategy

1. Ensure that the association's priorities are clearly defined and agreed upon using a sound decision-making process. Recognize that strategy follows objectives. The concentration decision is arguably the board's most important contribution.

2. Participate in establishing performance measurements for each priority goal or objective. Once the direction is set and the areas for concentration defined, the board must hold the CEO and itself accountable for follow-through and execution. Performance measurements are essential. Everybody needs to know how the association is doing in order to measure progress. Everybody needs to know how the association is keeping score.

3. Hold the CEO accountable for achieving established performance measures.

4. Participate in crafting strategy, but remember that once it is defined, the CEO owns it until it needs an overhaul.

5. Constructively challenge emerging strategy, asking difficult questions, both of themselves and of the CEO. One of the best ways for a director to contribute is to ask good questions.

6. Support strategy by approving budgets, necessary investments, and other resource allocations. A basic function of a board is to ensure that the organization has adequate operating resources. Unfunded mandates are irresponsible. Boards need to provide the resources required or scale back programs to match the resources available.

7. Complete an annual assessment with the CEO and, if appropriate, senior staff of performance in the association's adoption of the five strategies for competitiveness along with gains made in the technology arena.

8. Create a sense of urgency around strategy implementation. This sense of urgency is often lacking in change or transformation efforts, but the road to relevance is a fast track. Every day of delay puts the association further behind.

9. Avoid activities or directives that divert the association from its strategic direction. Many boards are inclined to want to do it all instead of limiting activities. The competitive environment will be very unkind to the association that doesn't exercise restraint and self-control.

10. Direct committees and task forces to align their work with the strategies. Committee chairs can have minds of their own. Since they don't have to worry about anything but their committee, they can be prone to resist direction, preferring to go their own way with their own ideas. Sometimes this can produce remarkable results. But in our experience, it rarely does. Boards must give committees tight charges consistent with the association's strategic direction. When possible, boards should use the task force model with a specific charge and a limited time for achieving the best results with today's volunteers. This tactic not only responds to the time pressures faced by members but also increases the chances of getting tightly focused proposals and suggestions.

Afterword

Though the competitive environment is rapidly changing, one of the strengths of associations is the camaraderie among members. We don't see this changing. There will always be the desire—and the need—for individuals to share common problems, commiserate, collaborate, and work to advance their profession or industry. What is changing is how they will do it.

We believe it's an exciting time to be in association management and governance—either as staff or a volunteer. Much is changing but change means opportunity. The associations that journey the road to relevance are more likely to weather the new normal. In the end, we believe they will:

Be more disciplined. By design, the strategies in this book will create more deliberate and intentional decision-making processes for associations. The end result will be adequately resourced and more narrowly focused products and services, a benefit for both the association and its members.

Be more entrepreneurial. Increased competition requires a new way of thinking. Though associations are typically conservative by nature, the market recognizes and rewards cutting-edge risk takers. We don't believe this has to be careless risk taking. But we do believe that a more entrepreneurial approach will be necessary.

Be more businesslike. With member loyalty waning and the internet calling, the association is no longer the first stop for members when they need assistance. This means that associations are going to have to be more like for-profit companies in their approaches to creating value to get—and keep—member attention. By necessity, the use of tools such as market research, marketing expertise, and online commerce will have to increase.

Be more technology driven. Technology is changing our world daily—and sometimes instantly. How can your association compete with that? Increasingly, the answer is going to be "via more technology." The bad news is that technology requires financial resources and expertise that many associations don't have. The good news is that you personally don't have to understand it, know how to deploy it, or even be able to anticipate what's coming next. You just have to find someone who can do this for you, whether on staff or in a consultant role. The strategies in this book will help you find the financial resources necessary to get and keep you in the technology game. As a reminder, the strategies are:

- Build on strength.
- Concentrate resources.
- Integrate programs and services.
- Align people and processes for efficiency.
- Abandon services and activities when necessary.

The above strategies help minimize detours on the road to relevance. The secret to success is recognizing what relevance looks like for your association and what it will take to create and maintain it for your members. It's different for every association. Set your course based on your situation and be willing to make adjustments along the way. Relevance isn't static. Associations must be both bold and nimble on the road to relevance.

Associations that have relevance in the future will be strategic in responding to increased competition and the new normal. The road may be long but the rewards are worth it.

APPENDIX A
Resources

These resources will help you learn more about lean processes:

- Mike Rother and John Shook. *Learning to See: Value Stream Mapping to Add Value and Eliminate MUDA.* Lean Enterprise Institute, 1999.

- Beau Keyte and Drew Locher, *The Complete Lean Enterprise: Value Stream Mapping for Administrative and Office Processes.* Productivity Press, 2004.

- Mary Walton. *The Deming Management Method.* The Putnam Publishing Group, 1986.

Program and Service Evaluation Matrix

The following matrix was designed to assist associations in a critical evaluation of their programs, services and activities. The "forced choice" approach eliminates the tendency to give high ratings across the board and the numerical assessment is intended to reduce bias and emotions.

Program, service, product, or activity	Relatedness to mission	Life cycle position	Percentage of members use	Financial results or potential	Effective use of staff and volunteer time	Available from other sources?	Would we start today?	Total

List all association programs, products, services, and activities in the first vertical column. (Sometimes just putting this list together will be illuminating.) Larger, more complex associations may have to do this by department.

Total the number of all programs, services, products, and activities. Divide the total by 5 for your "rating quota." For example, if you have 30 programs and services listed, divide by 5 and your rating quota is 6. The quota limits the number of programs you can give high rankings and forces you to give lower rankings.

Under each vertical column heading, you should assign a number from 1 to 5 to each program or service. A "5" is the highest or most favorable rating, and a "1" is the lowest. However, you must assign ratings limited by your rating quota. In the example above with 30 programs and services, you can give only six programs a "5" rating, six programs a "4" rating, and so on. (Yes, six programs must be given a "1.") We recommend that you fill in the six "5s" first, then the six "1s." Then fill in six "4s," and finally the six "2s" and six "3s."

Total the ratings horizontally and rank them from the highest total to the lowest using an Excel spreadsheet. Ask why you are continuing the programs and services in the lower third of the evaluation.

Using the matrix will enable you to make an objective comparison of products and services without worrying about the sacred cows and political land mines that often keep associations from evaluating their offerings and eliminating those that have outlived their usefulness or never lived up to their potential. Doing so frees up valuable resources in both finances and human resources.

Endnotes

1. Martin Reeves, Claire Love, and Philipp Tillmanns, "Your Strategy Needs a Strategy." *Harvard Business Review,* September 2012. 2.

2. Peter Drucker. *Management: Tasks, Responsibilities, Practices.* Harper Business, 1993. 104.

3. Ibid. 119.

4. Ian Davis. http://www.mckinseyquarterly.com/The_new_normal_2326. Accessed September 14, 2012.

5. Arthur C. Brooks. "Generations and the Future of Association Participation." William E. Smith Institute for Association Research, 2006. 15.

6. Davis. op. cit.

7. Jim Collins. *Good to Great.* Harper Business, 2001. 205.

8. Jean Van Rensselar. "Focus on What You Do Best," *Distributor Focus,* August 2011. B.

9. Marcus Buckingham and Donald O. Clifton. *Now, Discover Your Strengths.* Simon and Schuster, 2001. 58.

10. Harrison Coerver and Mary Byers, *Race for Relevance: 5 Radical Changes for Associations.* ASAE, 2011. 140.

11. Ibid.

12. Chris Zook and James Allen. *Profit from the Core.* Harvard Business Review Press, 2010. 17.

13. C.K. Prahalad and Gary Hamel. "The Core Competence of the Corporation," *Harvard Business Review,* May 1990. 83.

14. Collins. op. cit. 90–91.

15. Collins. op. cit. 95–96.

16. Marcus Buckingham. *Find Your Strongest Life.* Thomas Nelson, 2009. 163.

17. Van Rensselar. op. cit. D.

18. Zook. op. cit. 19.

19. Drucker. op. cit. 785.

20. Collins. op. cit. 114.

21. Carl Von Clausewitz. *On War: The Complete Edition.* Wildside Press LLC, 2009. 204.

22. Chris Zook. As quoted in Walter Kiechel III. *The Lords of Strategy.* Harvard Business School Press, 2010. 284.

23. Drucker. op. cit. 104.

24. Ibid. 105.

25. Ibid. 123.

26. Henry Mintzberg. "The Fall and Rise of Strategic Planning," *Harvard Business Review,* January/February, 1994. 107.

27. Ibid.

28. Glenn Tecker. "The Future of Planning for the Future," *Associations Now,* April/May 2012, Vol. 8 Issue 4. 27–31.

29. Peter Drucker. *The Effective Executive.* Harper Collins, 1967. xv.

30. Joe Rominiecki. Acroynym blog, http://blogs.asaecenter.org/Acronym/2012/02/what_do_associations_do_better.html. Accessed October 25, 2012.

31. Louis E. Boone and David L. Kurtz. *Contemporary Business, Edition 13.* John Wiley & Sons, 2010.

32. John Kao. As quoted in Mark Athitakis. "A Fine-Tuned Innovation Culture," *Associations Now,* February 2012. 40–41.

33. Kim S. Nash. "2011 State of the CIO." *CIO,* January 2011. 32.

34. World War II: D-Day, The Invasion of Normandy, The Dwight D. Eisenhower Presidential Library and Museum, http://eisenhower.archives.gov/research/online_documents/d_day.html. Accessed September 19, 2012.

35. Michael Porter. "What is Strategy?" *Harvard Business Review,* November/December 1996. 13.

36. Joan Magretta. "Jim Collins, Meet Michael Porter." (*Harvard Business Review* blog network, December 15, 2011). http://blogs.hbr.org/cs/2011/12/jim_collins_meet_michael_porte.html.

37. "Author John Grisham Has No Shortage of Book Ideas," *The Phillippine Daily Inquirer,* September 1, 2008.
http://showbizandstyle.inquirer.net/breakingnews/breakingnews/view/20080901-157978/Author-John-Grisham-has-no-shortage-of-book-ideas. Accessed September 14, 2012.

38. Alison Flood. "Potter Tops 400 Million Sales." http://www.thebookseller.com/news/potter-tops-400-million-sales.html, June 17, 2008. Accessed September 14, 2012.

39. "John Grisham Wins Galaxy Award." http://www.writerswrite.com/blog/329071, March 29, 2007. Accessed September 14, 2012.

40. Walter Kiechel III. *The Lords of Strategy.* Harvard Business School Press, 2010. 252.

41. Michael Porter. op. cit. 13.

42. Ibid.

43. Paul Leinwand and Cesare Mainardi. "The Coherence Premium," *Harvard Business Review,* June 2010. 90.

44. Coerver and Byers. op. cit. 141–142.

45. Susan Besze Wallace. "The Mettle of Metal," *Forum,* September 2011. 14.

46. FMI Corporation. Study about use of metal in buildings. 2010.

47. Mark Engle. As quoted in Wallace. op. cit. 14.

48. Alan Shalloway, Guy Beaver, and James R. Trott. *Lean-Agile Software Development: Achieving Enterprise Agility.* Addison-Wesley, 2009.

49. Porter. op. cit. 15.

50. Kiechel III. op. cit. xii.

51. Jaynie L. Smith and William G. Flanagan. *Creating Competitive Advantage.* Crown Business, 2006. 92.

52. Sarah L. Sladek. *The End of Membership as We Know It.* ASAE, 2011.

53. Smith and Flanagan. op. cit. 145.

54. Adrian J. Slywotzky. *Value Migration: How to Think Several Moves Ahead of the Competition.* Harvard Business Review Press, 1995. 4.

55. James P. Womack and Daniel T. Jones. *Lean Solutions: How Companies and Customers Can Create Value and Wealth Together.* Simon & Shuster Free Press, 2005. 5–6.

56. Jamie Turner. The 60 Second Marketer. http://60secondmarketer.com/blog/2011/10/18/more-mobile-phones-than-toothbrushes/. Accessed November 23, 2012.

57. Peter Drucker. "Managing for Business Effectiveness." *Harvard Business Review,* March 1963. 53–60.

58. Cynthia Karen Swank. "The Lean Service Machine." *Harvard Business Review,* October 2003. 129.

59. Eric Ries. *The Lean Startup: How Today's Entrepreneurs Use Continuous Innovation to Create Radically Successful Businesses.* Random House, 2011. 284.

60. Taiichi Ohno. *Toyota Production System: Beyond Large-Scale Production.* Productivity Press, 1988.

61. W. Edwards Deming. *Out of Crisis.* MIT Press, 1982. 53.

62. ASAE. *Operating Ratio Report.* 14th Edition. 2012. 102.

63. Susan Cane. *Quiet: The Power of Introverts in a World That Can't Stop Talking.* Random House, 2012.

64. James Dalton and Monica Digman. *The Decision to Join.* ASAE, 2007.

65. ASAE. *Benchmarking in Association Management: Financial Operations Policies and Procedures (Volume 6).* 2012.

66. BoardSource Nonprofit Governance Index 2010. https://www.boardsource.org/dl.asp?document_id=884. Accessed December 1, 2012.

67. Ries. op. cit. 284.

68. Womack and Jones. op. cit. 52.

69. Roger Gill. *Theory and Practice of Leadership.* SAGE Publications Ltd., 2006. 8.

70. Walter Isaacson. *Steve Jobs.* Simon & Schuster, 2011. 337.

71. Ibid.

72. Ibid. 338.

73. Peter Drucker. *Managing the Nonprofit Organization: Principles and Practices.* Harper Collins, 1990. 158.

74. John Carver. *Boards that Make a Difference: A New Design for Leadership in Nonprofit and Public Organizations.* Third Edition. Jossey-Bass, 2006. 48–50.

Acknowledgements

The authors would like to thank the following people who shared information about their association or encouraged us in some way while we worked on the manuscript:

David Bergman

Gary Bolinger, CAE

Stuart Byers

April Collins

Peter DuBois

Quinn Dufurrena

Peggy Dzierzawski, CAE

Drew Eason, CAE

Mark Engle, CAE

Taylor Fernley

Mike Fisher, CAE

Sandra Fisher, CAE

Dorothy Fragaszy

Natascha Fronczek

Mike Garcia

Bob Harris, CAE

Nancy Honeycutt, CAE

Tim Jackson, CAE

Rick Klein

Holly Koenig

Gary LaBranche, CAE

Josh Lord

Lori Maarschalk

Carol Meerschaert

Tom Morrison

Buddy Patrick

Elizabeth Price, CAE

Marilen Reimer, CAE

Doug Reinhardt

Martha Reinhardt

Nancy Rummel

Bob Rusbuldt

Peggy Savage

Greg Sax

Karen Scarpella

Diane Scheuring, CAE

Will Sears

Keith Skillman, CAE

Wade Smith

Emily Stegman

Leonard Toenjes, CAE

Mark Tomlinson

Judith Trepeck

Lezlee Westine

Baron Williams, CAE

Gregory Williams

William Zepp, CAE

Special thanks to Shawn Montgomery for handling research for this project.

(Note: Only ASAE credentials current as of December 2012 are included on this list.)

About the Authors

HARRISON COERVER is president of Harrison Coerver & Associates, a management consulting firm specializing in trade associations, professional societies, and other tax-exempt membership organizations. Since 1985, Coerver has consulted with more than 1,000 associations in strategy, planning, marketing, and management. He is known for his group facilitation skills, straightforward style, and innovative approaches to association governance and management. He is also a frequent speaker and seminar leader on future trends for associations and professional societies and is a former member of the board of directors of the Association Forum of Chicagoland, a 4,000-member organization serving association professionals in the greater Chicago area.

Coerver is the author of articles for many association publications, including *Associations Now, Forum,* and *Association Trends.* In addition to writing, he conducted the research for the American Society of Association Executives Foundation's study, "Critical Competencies for Association Executives."

Coerver is an honorary member of the Texas Society of Association Executives, an Allied Member of the Year at the Kansas City Society of Association Executives, and a recipient of the Association Forum of Chicagoland's Organizational Service Award, and he has been recognized by the Tennessee Society of Association Executives for his contributions to association management.

Subscribe to his newsletter, *Association News and Views,* at www. harrisoncoerver.com, or contact him at harrison@harrisoncoerver.com.

MARY BYERS, CAE is a former association executive and has been a professional speaker and strategic planning facilitator since 1988. She consults with organizations about developing leadership potential, creating harmony in work teams, developing strategic plans, and initiating and managing tough conversations. She's a member of the National Speakers Association and has presented in 28 states on a variety of topics. Byers is also the author of seven commercially published books and has contributed to *Associations Now* and many state association newsletters.

Byers is the former director of communications and member services at the Illinois State Dental Society and director of advertising for the for-profit division of the International Order of the Golden Rule, an international trade association. She is a member of both the American and Illinois Societies of Association Executives.

Byers is the recipient of the Association Excellence and President's Awards from the Illinois Society of Association Executives and was named Big Sister of the Year by Big Brothers/Big Sisters of Sangamon County. She was also a 2010 nominee for the Springfield Chamber of Commerce's Athena Award, which recognizes contributions to women's leadership potential, professional development, and quality of life.

Subscribe to Mary's newsletter, *Associations Today,* at www.marybyers. com, or contact her at mbyers@marybyers.com.

To learn more about *Race for Relevance* or *Road to Relevance,* including downloading free matrices, go to www.roadtorelevance.com.

Index

Ries, Eric, 101, 110
ROF, *see* Return on Fit
Rominiecki, Joe, 53
Rother, Mike, 149
Rummel, Nancy, 157
Rusbuldt, Bob, 157

S

Savage, Peggy, 157
Scarpella, Karen, 157
Scheuring, CAE, Diane, 157
Schick-Wilkinson Sword, 83
Sears, Will, 31, 157
Services provided by associations, *see*
  also Programs and services offered by
  associations
    certification, 29
    educational, 28–29
    fit rating, 86–87
    service suites, 81, 97
Shook, John, 149
Skillman, CAE, Keith, 157
Sladek, Sarah, 95
Slywotzky, Adrian J., 97
  value migration, 97
SME, *see* Society of Manufacturing Engineers
Smith, Jaynie L., 94, 95
Smith, Wade, 157
Social media and associations, 45–46
Society of Manufacturing Engineers (SME),
  Case Study, 39–40
Staffing of associations, 4–5
Stegman, Emily, 157
Strategic planning, 50–53
  board involvement, 51–52
  fit criteria, 87
  Mintzberg, Henry, 51
  redundancies, 107
  streamlining functions, 108–109
  value stream mapping, 111, 112, 116–117,
    Appendix A
  waste management, 102–105
Strategic thinking, 52–53, 148
  continuous improvement, 112–113,
    Appendix A
  lean thinking, 94, 101–102, 115,
    Appendix A
    human capital, 104–105
    "seven wastes," 102–104
  product abandonment, 119–120
  senior staff, 52
  value, defining, 94–95

T–U

Technology and associations, 3, 5, 61, 84, 148
Tecker, Glenn, 53
Texas Trial Lawyers Association (TTLA), 17,
  83–84
    TrialSmith®, 83–84
Tillmanns, Philipp, v
Time pressures, 2
Toenjes, CAE, Len, 136, 137, 158
Tomlinson, CEO, Mark, 39, 40, 158
Timmons, Jay, 56
Trepeck, Judith, 158
TTLA, *see* Texas Trial Lawyers Association

V

Value
  attributes of customer value, 97–99
  defining, 110–111
  determining, 95
  expectations, 2, 96–97
  threshold question, 96–97
  value migration, 97
Value Migration: How to Think Several Moves
  Ahead of the Competition, 97
Van Rensselar, Jean, 8, 28
Visiting Nurse Association of Florida (VNA),
  95
Volunteer dynamic, 63
von Clausewitz, 41, 67

W–Y

Walton, Mary, 149
Welch, Jack, 35
Westine, Lezlee, 158
Williams, CAE, Baron, 158
Williams, Gregory, 158
Womack, James P., 97, 111
Wozniak, Steve, 123

Z

Zepp, CAE, William, 158
Zook, Chris, 24, 28, 48, 74
  2004 growth survey, 48